Thomas Schirrmacher

Missio Dei

World of Theology Series

Published by the Theological Commission of the World Evangelical Alliance

Volume 10

Vol 1	Thomas K. Johnson: The First Step in Missions Training: How our Neighbors are Wrestling with God's General Revelation
Vol 2	Thomas K. Johnson: Christian Ethics in Secular Cultures
Vol 3	David Parker: Discerning the Obedience of Faith: A Short History of the World Evangelical Alliance Theological Commission
Vol 4	Thomas Schirrmacher (Ed.): William Carey: Theologian – Linguist – Social Reformer
Vol 5	Thomas Schirrmacher: Advocate of Love – Martin Bucer as Theologian and Pastor
Vol 6	Thomas Schirrmacher: Culture of Shame / Culture of Guilt
Vol 7	Thomas Schirrmacher: The Koran and the Bible
Vol 8	Thomas Schirrmacher (Ed.): The Humanisation of Slavery in the Old Testament
Vol 9	Jim Harries: New Foundations for Appreciating Africa: Beyond Religious and Secular Deceptions
Vol 10	Thomas Schirrmacher: Missio Dei – God's Missional Nature
Vol 11	Thomas Schirrmacher: Biblical Foundations for 21st Century World Mission

Thomas Schirrmacher

Missio Dei
God's Missional Nature

Translated by Richard McClary

Edited by Thomas K. Johnson

Assisted by Bruce Barron

WIPF & STOCK · Eugene, Oregon

Wipf and Stock Publishers
199 W 8th Ave, Suite 3
Eugene, OR 97401

Missio Dei
God's Missional Nature
By Schirrmacher, Thomas
Copyright©2017 Verlag für Kultur und Wissenschaft
ISBN 13: 978-1-5326-5578-4
Publication date 4/17/2018
Previously published by Verlag für Kultur und Wissenschaft, 2017

Contents

The origins of this book 7

1 Introduction: Historical Missiology 9
   On the History of the Term 9
   The Uncashed Check 12
   Missio Dei as a Catchword in Opposition to Missions: a Consequence of a Missing Explanation 16

2 Biblical-Systematic Section 19
   An "Orthodox" Concept? 19
   Sending in the New Testament 20
   God, the First Missionary 33
   Excursus: Sending in the Old Testament 34
   Jesus, the Missionary Par Excellence 36
   Jesus Receives Everything from His Father 37
   The Holy Spirit as Missionary (John 16:5–14) 39
   Excursus: God Comes Near to Us – on Differences between the Bible and the Koran 41
   Pentecost: Missio Dei Par Excellence 42
   We are Enlisted – not in spite of but rather on account of the Holy Spirit 44
   The Unsuited Individual 47
   Belief Comes through Preaching: Romans 10:14–17 51
   Love and Missio Dei 52
   Excursus: The Dual Concept of the Apostle in the New Testament 56

3 Confessional Section 65
   The Filioque: Son and Spirit 65
   Missio Dei and Orthodox Theology 74
   Missio Dei and Catholic Theology 75

Appendix: On the Term "Missional" 79
About the Author 85

The origins of this book

This book started as a guest lecture at the STH Basel, a private university in Switzerland, on October 21, 2004. The occasion was an event honoring **Eberhard Troeger** for his longstanding involvement in missions in the Islamic world. The lecture later appeared in a Festschrift for Troeger.[1] Many of the statements made in the lecture are documented here in detail. I find the topic so important that I have made it a fixed component of my missiology lectures since 1983.[2] I have defined the topic as follows in a lexicon:

> "The term *missio Dei* (from Latin, meaning "God's mission") has meant the inner-Trinitarian process of sending, originally found in Catholic dogmatics and particularly since St. Augustine. The World Missionary Conference held in Willingen in 1952 adopted the term for the Protestant realm in order to illustrate that world missions efforts are rooted in the Trinitarian nature of God. Georg F. Vicedom made the term popular through his book *Missio Dei* (1958). In the New Testament, the sending of the disciples by Jesus is understood to be an extension of the sending of Jesus by his Father (Matthew 10:40; Mark 9:37; Luke 9:48; 10:16; Acts 3:20, 26; approx. 50 times in John; comp. as far back as in the Old Testament, Isaiah 48:16) and the sending of the Holy Spirit by the Father and Jesus (John 14:26; 15:26; Luke 24:49) and for that reason uses the same words for 'to send,' 'sending,' etc. (Latin: *missio*) (particularly John 17:18; 20:21)."[3]

This topic is particularly fruitful for the complementarian approach to dogmatics that we recommend, since Christian revelation and Biblical doctrine demonstrate particularly striking complementarity when it comes to the missio Dei. On one hand, the missio Dei means that God has done everything and does everything, and without him every mission is in vain. On the other hand, the missio Dei does not make the individual

---

[1] Thomas Schirrmacher, "Missio Dei," in *Mission im Islam: Festschrift für Eberhard Troeger*, ed. Klaus W. Müller (Nuremberg: VTR; Bonn: VKW, 2007), 165–88.

[2] Compare my earlier articles "Missio Dei" and "God, the First Missionary," *Reflection: An International Reformed Review of Missiology* 5, nos. 1–2 (Sept/Nov 1994): 38–41 = "'Missio Dei' – God the First Missionary," *Chalcedon Report* 352 (Nov 1994): 29–31; "Missio Dei: Missiologische Begriffe kurz erläutert," (6) *Evangelikale Missiologie* 9 (1993): 110.

[3] Thomas Schirrmacher, "Lexikon des Christentums," in *Harenberg Lexikon der Religionen* (Düsseldorf: Harenberg Verlag, 2002), 196 (keyword "Missio Dei").

Christian superfluous or leave Christians without any responsibilities. Rather, by being sent, people and the church receive the greatest mandate that exists on earth.

I Introduction: Historical Missiology

Preliminary remark: Whoever is primarily interested in the biblical-exegetical and systematic presentation can skip this section and begin at the heading "Biblical-systematic Section."

> "Mission is not the mission of the church but rather God's mission. And it is this way because mission is a predicate of God. God is a missionizing God. ... Missio Dei is active throughout all of history, and it consists in God's orienting himself towards the entire world, in as well as outside of the church. God guides the world through the events of history."[4]

On the History of the Term

In dogmatics, the Latin expression *missio* (sending out or mission)[5] originally meant the inner-Trinitarian process of sending. It was coined in the 4th century A.D. by St. Augustine to denote the sending of the Son by the Father and the sending of the Spirit by the Father and the Son, or the proceeding of the Son and the Spirit from the Father.[6] The term also plays a role in Orthodox theology.[7] Subsequent to St. Augustine, it also became a technical term used by St. Thomas Aquinas for Trinitarian doctrine, having to do with the eternal procession of the Son and the Spirit

---

[4] "Bischof Birkeli, Norwegen," quoted in Anna Marie Aagaard, "Missio Dei in katholischer Sicht: Missionstheologische Tendenzen," *Evangelische Theologie* 34 (1974): 421.

[5] See Karl Müller, *Missionstheologie* (Berlin: D. Reimer, 1985), 57–59; Horst Rzepkowski, *Lexikon der Mission* (Graz: Sytria, 1992), 296 (keyword *missio Dei*); Hans-Werner Gensichen, *Glaube für die Welt: Theologische Aspekte der Mission* (Gütersloh: Gütersloher Verlagshaus, 1971), 55–57; Lesslie Newbigin, *The Relevance of Trinitarian Doctrine for Today's Mission* (Edinburgh: Edinburgh House Press, 1963), 31–34.

[6] Compare Augustinus Edward W. Poitras, "St. Augustine and the Missio Dei: A Reflection on Mission at the Close of the Twentieth Century," *Mission Studies* 16 (1999): 26–46; also, www.sant-agostino.it/ricerca/index.htm, then enter "missio" as the search, for thousands of results for *missio Filii Dei* (often together with incarnation), *missio Spiritus Sancti*, etc.

[7] See additional confirming instances from other church fathers in Johann Auer and Joseph Ratzinger, *Kleine katholische Dogmatik*, vol. 2: *Gott, der Eine und Dreieine* (Regensburg: Friedrich Pustet, 1978) 295–304.

from God and the historical sending of the Son and the Spirit.[8] However, with respect to these two theological giants and in spite of the enormous significance of *missio* as an inner-Trinitarian process, these definitions did not refer to the *missio* on the part of Jesus' disciples. That use of the terminology of *missio* came only later in history.

By the middle of the 16th century, for reasons that remain unknown, Ignatius of Loyola used *missio* instead of the terms used previously to refer to promoting the Christian faith (e.g., *propaganda*), whereby this Latin term then found its way primarily into Spanish (*mision*) and Portuguese (*missao*). The Portuguese had used the term since the middle of the 15th century as a political term for the sending of people overseas. It is disputed whether the term referred to papal authorization for Ignatius' political 'missio' or if the thought that has to do with the dissemination of the gospel worldwide.[9]

In Latin, *missio* means to dispatch, to send off, to set loose, to release, to let go of, say farewell to, refrain from, or conclude.[10] Not until after the Reformation did it receive the special meaning in medieval Church Latin of Christian sending, following the roots of the Greek word for *apostle* and the Greek words for sending out the messengers of Christ. The German word *Mission* "appears for the first time in German texts in the 16th century with the same general meaning as the Latin word. Since the 17th century, Church Latin – as well as other languages of culture – has conveyed the common and general meaning of the word in the sense of ('the sending out of Christian heralds for') converting heathens."[11] At the end of the 18th century came the adoption of the meaning from French as a message from a country, and then the secularization of the term so that it took on the general meaning of a mandate or duty. As derivations of *Mission*, one can see the form *Missionar* (German word for missionary), added

---

[8] On Thomas Aquinas, go to www.corpusthomisticum.org/it/index.age, then enter *missio* as the search, for 686 results for missio filii, missio spiritus sancti, missio filii vel spiritus sancti, missionis tres personae, etc.

[9] I here follow the in-depth investigation by Paul Kollmann, "At the Origins of Mission and Missiology," *Journal of the American Academy of Religion* 79:2, 425-458, spring 2011.

[10] For instance, see "Missio," col. 1764 in Karl Ernst Georges, *Kleines Lateinisch-Deutsches Handwörterbuch* (Hannover and Leipzig: Hahn, 1909); most comprehensively, "Missio," col. 1139-41 in: *Thesaurus linguae latinae*, vol. 8 (Leipzig: Teubner), 1936-56.

[11] "Mission," in *Duden: Das Herkunftswörterbuch*, vol. 7 (Mannheim: Dudenverlag, 2007), 532; "Mission," in *Ethymologisches Wörterbuch des Deutschen* (Munich: DTV, 2005), 877.

1 Introduction: Historical Missiology

from the 17th century onwards, while *missionieren* (German word meaning to conduct missionary work) was added in the 19th century.

In the wake of the World Missionary Conference held in Willingen in 1952, which emphasized the Trinitarian justification of world missions,[12] the term *missio Dei* was adopted by Karl Hartenstein and Walter Freytag for the Protestant realm[13] to portray the fact that world missions work is rooted in God as Trinity. The term *missio Dei* was not found at Willingen itself. Rather, it first appeared in Hartenstein's report on Willingen.[14] The Trinitarian justification of mission itself was, however, already a topic at Willingen.[15] Hartenstein[16] writes: "Mission is not only obedience towards a word of the Lord. It is not only a duty for gathering the church. It is participation in the sending of the Son, of the 'missio Dei' with its comprehensive goal of establishing the rule of Christ over the entire creation."[17]

---

[12] Compare the conference on the 50-year anniversary of Willingen: Evangelisches Missionswerk in Deutschland, ed., "Mission Dei heute: Zur Aktualität eines missiologischen Schlüsselbegriffs," *Weltmission heute* 52 (Hamburg: EMW, 2002).

[13] Karl Hartenstein, "Theologische Besinnung," in *Mission zwischen Gestern und Morgen*, ed. Walter Freytag (Stuttgart: Ev. Missionsverlag, 1952), 51–72 (Willingen 1952 proceedings).

[14] H. H. Rosin, *"Missio Dei:" An Examination of the Origin, Contents and Function of the Term in Protestant Missiological Discussion* (Leiden: Interuniversitair Instituut voor Missiologie en Oecumenica, 1972) 6–7 [comp. the Dutch original: *Missio Dei, Kern en Functie in de Zendings – theologische Discussie* (Leiden, 1971)]. According to Theo Sundermeier, "Missio Dei heute: Zur Identität christlicher Mission," *Theologische Literaturzeitung* 127 (2002): col. 1243, the topic arose "only incidentally" at Willingen.

[15] Rosin, *Missio Dei*, 10-19; Wilhelm Richebächer, "Missio Dei: The Basis of Mission Theology or a Wrong Path?" *International Review of Mission*, volume 92, issue 367, 588–605, October 2003; Tormod Engelsviken, "Verständnis und Missverständnis eines Theologischen Begriffes in den Europäischen Kirchen und der Europäischen Missionstheologie," 35-57 in Evangelisches Missionswerk in Deutschland (ed.), "Mission Dei heute: Zur Aktualität eines missiologischen Schlüsselbegriffs," *Weltmission heute* 52 (Hamburg: EMW, 2002), 36-37.

[16] On Hartenstein, see Wolfgang Metzger (ed.), *Karl Hartenstein: Ein Leben für Kirche und Mission* (Stuttgart: Ev. Missionsverlag, 1953), especially the article by Walter Freytag et al., "Mitglied im Deutschen Evangelischen Missionsrat und Missionstag und bei den Tagungen der Ökumene," 293–312; Fritz H. Lamparter (ed.), *Karl Hartenstein – Leben in weltweitem Horizont: Beiträge zu seinem 100. Geburtstag* (Bonn: Verlag für Kultur und Wissenschaft, 1995).

[17] Karl Hartenstein, "Theologische Besinnung," 54, quoted in Georg F. Vicedom, *Missio Dei* (Munich: Chr. Kaiser, 1958), 12 (new edition – see next comment – p. 32).

Georg F. Vicedom made the term known as a third Lutheran missiologist, along with Hartenstein and Freytag, in 1958 through his book *Missio Dei*.[18] Vicedom summarizes:

> "Missio Dei is a term used in Catholic dogmatics, which is meant to describe the inner-Trinitarian events of sending. The Father sends the Son. The Father and the Son send the Holy Spirit for the salvation of humanity. The World Missionary Conference held in Willingen in 1952 adopted the term in order to substantiate missionary theology within Protestant Christianity as actions taken by the Trinitarian God. Since that time, it has largely determined the thinking in Protestant missionary theology. Missio Dei declares God's sending to be God's own cause, which began with his own Son and which he will continue in his church up to the end of time. With that, the mission of the church is linked to God's mission itself. Thus the church stands in God's service for the dissemination of his gospel. It cannot be God's church if it does not participate in the sending of the Son. Mission thus becomes a basic function of the church. However, it would be a stricture on missio Dei if one wanted to only restrict the term to sending. What also belongs to the term is everything which has to be done for the sake of the announcement of salvation and what God does – calling, preparation, sending of the workers as well as the accomplishment of their varied services. All of these items belong to the realization of the love of God as determined by missio."[19]

The Uncashed Check

Hartenstein and even Vicedom never cashed the wonderful check that they issued. While perhaps in the case of Hartenstein this is traceable back to the brevity of his texts, this is not the case with Vicedom, who wrote whole books on the topic. In his case, in spite of everything he wrote, there are missing exegetical and systematic statements about the

---

[18] Vicedom's works *Missio Dei* and *Actio Dei* have now been published by Klaus W. Müller in one volume: Georg Vicedom, *Missio Dei – Actio Dei* (Nürnberg: VTR, 2002). Vicedom's life and work as a missionary in New Guinea and his theology up to World War II are described in Klaus W. Müller, "Peacemaker: Missionary Practice of Georg Friedrich Vicedom in New Guinea (1929–1939)," dissertation, University of Aberdeen, 1993 (UMI/University Microfilms), now published as Klaus W. Müller, *Georg F. Vicedom as Missionary and Peacemaker* (Erlangen: Erlanger Verlag für Mission und Ökumene, 2003).

[19] Georg F. Vicedom, "Missio Dei," in *Lexikon der Weltmission*, ed. Stephen Neill, Niels-Peter Moritzen, and Ernst Schrupp (Wuppertal: R. Brockhaus; Erlangen: Verlag der Evang.-Luth. Mission, 1975), 352.

1 Introduction: Historical Missiology

Trinity, about the inner-Trinitarian relationship as it relates to sending, about the link between God as the sent one to people as messengers, and about the relationship of the Spirit of God, who has been conducting missions since Pentecost, to the missionary activity of the church and its members. Also missing is a justification of how one moves to the topic of the Kingdom of God from the missio Dei.[20]

In Vicedom's "Actio Dei," the topic of missio Dei arises only incidentally as a requirement and accounts for less than one percent of the text.[21] Indeed, it is the topic of the kingdom of God which is considered exegetically, systematically, and missiologically throughout the entire book. In *Missio Dei*, the topic itself accounts for less than 5% of the text.[22] Also, in this work one sees the kingdom of God elaborately considered and then apostleship comprehensively discussed, subjects that naturally stand in close relationship to teaching on missio Dei. However, it does not treat anything that would not be contained in any other missiological justification. Thus, Vicedom briefly indicates that "sending [is] an act of the love of God,"[23] but nowhere is anything explained about the love of God in relation to the Trinity or missions. In short, Henning Wrogemann is correct in saying that Vicedom's justification for missions lies in the kingdom of God and that, in contrast, missio Dei remains a pure postulation.[24] Ironically, the innumerable articles and other contributions on Vicedom's understanding of missio Dei seem to occupy more space than Vicedom himself devoted to the topic in all his many publications.

This criticism applies to many additional missiologists. Lesslie Newbigin, for example, in his important work entitled *The Relevance of Trinitarian Doctrine for Today's Mission*, dedicates only three pages of his book to the actual topic described in the title.[25] In the new edition of this book,[26]

---

[20] Henning Wrogemann, "Überlegungen zu Notwendigkeit und Problematik einer trinitarischen Begründung der Mission," Zeitschrift für Mission 28 (1997): 152, note 6: "Vicedom understands the Trinitarian justification of mission as an expression of the rule of God but, however, does not explain this consideration."
[21] Vicedom, Actio Dei, 124–25; in the new edition, Vicedom, Missio Dei - Actio Dei, 215–16.
[22] Vicedom, Missio Dei, 12–16, and briefly on pp. 39, 43; in the new edition, Vicedom. Missio Dei - Actio Dei, 32–36, and briefly on pp. 56, 59.
[23] Vicedom, Missio Dei, 39; in the new edition, 56.
[24] Wrogemann, "Überlegungen zu Notwendigkeit," 152.
[25] Newbigin, The Relevance of Trinitarian Doctrine for Today's Mission, 31–34. In his dissertation, Michael W. Goheen examines Newbigin's relationship to the Trinitarian justification for mission; see Goheen. "As the Father Has Sent Me, I Am Sending You": J. E. Lesslie Newbigin's Missionary Ecclesiology (Proefschrift: Universität Utrecht, 2001), 115–62, esp. 116–18 [downloadable as a pdf at

there is likewise little to be found. Indeed, at a later point, in 1989, he writes: "The mission of the church is to be understood, indeed it can only be understood, if it is described within the framework of a Trinitarian picture."[27] Nevertheless, he again considers the topic only briefly.[28]

Even articles with the title "Missio Dei" often contain no biblical-theological or systematic justification for God's sending or for the continuation of God's mission through the church. Rather, they often address other questions of missionary theology.[29] One gets the feeling that it is a matter of a trendy buzzword and that there is no actual interest in its content or substantive value.

Henning Wrogemann has expanded this criticism to additional theologians who basically plead for the concept of missio Dei, such as Hans-Werner Gensichen and Marc Spindler.[30] Horst Bürkle and Karl Müller do not even mention the concept once in their theologies of mission.[31] Even the positive example of Jürgen Moltmann,[32] which Wrogemann uses, is limited to a few sentences, albeit thorough and vital.[33]

Something similar applies to Karl Hartenstein and his teacher[34] Karl Barth. As early as his report on Willingen in 1952, Hartenstein dedicates

---

http://www.library.uu.nl/digiarchief/dip/diss/1947080/inhoud.htm]. Admittedly, his presentation takes up considerably more space than what Newbigin actually wrote on it. Newbigin later covered Trinitarian justification for mission in greater detail in *The Open Secret: Sketches for a Missionary Theology* (Grand Rapids, MI: Eerdmans; London: SPCK, 1978), and finally seminally in 1989 in *The Gospel in a Pluralistic Society* (Grand Rapids, MI: Eerdmans; Geneva: WCC Publications, 1989), but only on pp. 118-19, 134-35.

[26] Lesslie Newbigin, *Trinitarian Doctrine for Today's Mission* (Eugene, OR: Wipf & Stock, 1988).
[27] Ibid, 118.
[28] Ibid, 117-19, 123-24, 134-35.
[29] An example from the Third World is Abraham Christdhas, "Missio Dei," in *Work - Worship - Witness: Festschrift for Prof. Ken Gnanakan*, ed. Brian Wintle et al. (Bangalore: Theological Book Trust, 2003), 483-98.
[30] Wrogemann, "Überlegungen zu Notwendigkeit," 152-53.
[31] Ibid.
[32] Ibid., 153, referring to Jürgen Moltmann, *Kirche in der Kraft des Geistes* (Munich: Chr. Kaiser, 1975, 1989), 70; or more detail on missio in the Trinitarian teaching of Jürgen Moltmann, see *Trinität und Reich Gottes: Zur Gotteslehre* (Munich: Chr. Kaiser, 1986), 194-206.
[33] Wrogemann himself had expanded his 1997 article into "'Gott ist Liebe' - zu einer trinitarischen Begründung 'Missionarischer Identität' im Kontext des Pluralismus," *Zeitschrift für Mission* 29, no. 4 (2003): 295-313.
[34] Karl Hartenstein, "Was hat die Theologie Karl Barths der Mission zu sagen?" *Zwischen den Zeiten* 6 (1928): 59-83.

one to two pages to Missio Dei³⁵ while giving about ten times as much space to the kingdom of God.³⁶ At the same time, Hartenstein had already understood that in addition to his view at Willingen, there was also a view that equated the church with the kingdom of God and with the world in a way that masked eschatology.³⁷

According to Wrogemann, Barth had solidly anchored mission in missio Dei in his own way in a lecture held at the Brandenberg Missionary Conference on "Theology and Mission in Modern Times" in 1932. He thereby functioned as a stimulus but did not come back to the topic. Rather, he gave a covenantal justification of missions in his *Church Dogmatics*.³⁸ In 1932 Barth said:

> "Must not even the most faithful missionary, the most convinced friend of missions, have reason to reflect that the term *mission* was in the ancient Church an expression of the doctrine of the Trinity – namely the expression of the divine sending forth of self, the sending of the Son and Holy Spirit to the world? Can we indeed claim that we do it any other way?"³⁹

Ludwig Wiedenmann comments on this sentence as follows:

> "In this sentence a topic is struck upon which in the aftermath has been repeated innumerable times. That is the topic of missio Dei. In this the most radical relativization and at the same time the highest activation of all human and ecclesiastical action in missions is expressed. It is relativization because in the final event it is God who alone effects everything. It is activation because it is nevertheless service for the Word of God, who is continuously wanting to be active."⁴⁰

Here is a complete quotation of Barth's words:

> "What is mission? It surely is sought to be an activity of the church, even if it is only organizationally expressed indirectly. It is an activity of the church which wants to say: here is a particular form of confession towards

---

[35] Hartenstein, "Theologische Besinnung," 62–63.
[36] Ibid, 56, 67–68, 69, 71–72.
[37] Compare his criticism on pp. 68–71.
[38] Wrogemann, "Überlegungen zu Notwendigkeit," 153.
[39] Karl Barth, "Die Theologie und die Mission der Gegenwart," in Barth, *Theologische Fragen und Antworten. Gesammelte Vorträge 3* (Zollikon/Zürich: Evangelischer Verlag, 1957), 100 (from *Zwischen den Zeiten* [Munich: Chr. Kaiser, 1932]).
[40] Ludwig Wiedenmann, *Mission und Eschatologie: Eine Analyse der neueren deutschen evangelischen Missionstheologie* (Paderborn: Verlag Bonifacius-Druckerei, 1965), 66; see also Richebächer, "Missio Dei," 146.

God's self-revelation in Jesus Christ, a particular form of that human activity which seeks to understand itself as obedience to the call of Jesus Christ as Lord; an attempt to do his will, i.e., to orient his message, the message from him as the Lord, i.e., from the Creator, Reconciler, and Savior of man. It is this, that Jesus is in truth and reality this Lord and is the content of the Word of God, i.e., of the Word by which God speaks to man and that which the church wishes to serve by its actions. It is also that specifically which mission seeks to be in the church and with the church. This particular form, by which mission seeks to serve the Word of God, consists however, in the orientation of the message of Jesus Christ towards those people who are not yet in the church, i.e., those who do not yet confess to God's self-revelation in Jesus Christ, those who in any case have not heard his voice and who do not belong to him insofar as they are certainly without the unbreakable submissive dependency towards him and have not yet experienced the message-giving service of the church, have not yet had the visible confirming sign of baptism which is the will of God directed toward them. People under this rubric of 'not yet' are the heathens. Mission is and it seeks to be: the church which addresses itself to heathens and in this respect addresses itself outwards."[41]

Barth titled 250 pages of his *Church Dogmatics* with "The Holy Spirit and the Sending of the Christian Church"[42] but ultimately does not address the relationship between the sending of the Spirit and world missions, nor does he address missio Dei at this juncture.

Anna Marie Aagaard's straightforward claim that missio Dei is "new coinage which has its roots in Karl Barth's theology," the content of which was determined by "a Barthian student Karl Hartenstein" and a "Barth-inspired ecumenical seminar paper,"[43] seems rather one-sided to me, since the matter is addressed too briefly and almost at the periphery by Barth.

Missio Dei as a Catchword in Opposition to Missions: a Consequence of a Missing Explanation

The use of missio Dei as a slogan and the lack of detailed explanation of missio Dei in detail, even by its proponents, could be the main reason why he emphasis on missio Dei since Willingen has never really had

---

[41] Barth, "Die Theologie und die Mission der Gegenwart," 100–101.
[42] Karl Barth, *Kirchliche Dogmatik*, vol. 4 (Zürich: Theologischer Verlag, 1959), 3, § 72.
[43] Anna Marie Aagaard, "Missio Dei in katholischer Sicht," 421.

1 Introduction: Historical Missiology

much effect. It could also be the reason why missions moratoria and social gospel currents have appropriated this term too easily at and since Willingen.[44] The result is that missio Dei has mostly become an empty term unrelated to any effort to anchor missions in exegetical-systematic doctrines about the Trinity and salvation history. At the 3rd and 4th General Assemblies of the World Council of Churches (New Delhi 1961, Uppsala 1968), "missio Dei" became an expression for a completely new concept of missions in which, in the best-case scenario, the classical proclamation of the gospel played a subordinate role. Bernd Brandl justifiably makes the "vagueness"[45] of the term missio Dei responsible for the fact that in the end, at Uppsala in 1968, the humanization of the world was able to be seen as the embodiment of missio Dei, and even non-Evangelical missiologists offered ungentle reminders that missio Dei concepts that ignored the Trinity were preposterous.[46] This vagueness is not surprising when the term is not exegetically and systematically processed and filled with life but only remains a catchword.

Wilhelm Richebächer has demonstrated that despite all the significance of Willingen,[47] there were three parallel currents there: (1) the classic missionary viewpoint, above all that of German Lutheran mission theologians, (2) the "social gospel" view, above all from the USA, and (3) the call for a moratorium on missions coming from missionary countries for whom missio Dei means that missions are not a matter for the church but rather for God alone.[48] The slogan thus became so pervasive precisely because it was hardly filled with any content. If German Evangelicals in particular want to instinctively tie in nowadays with Hartenstein, Vicedom, and others, they have to be aware of this and catch up on their unfinished homework.

---

[44] A good overview of the various non-classical interpretations of missio Dei since 1952 and in particular in the 1960s and 1970s, by a non-evangelical critic of these developments, is offered by Tormod Engelsviken, "Verständnis und Missverständnis eines Theologischen Begriffes in den Europäischen Kirchen und der Europäischen Missionstheologie," 40–56; Richebächer, "Missio Dei," 148–61; Wrogemann, "Überlegungen zu Notwendigkeit," 154–67; Rosin, Missio Dei, 25–32.

[45] Bernd Brandl, "Mission und Reich Gottes," in Georg Vicedom, Missio Dei - Actio Dei, ed. Klaus W. Müller (Nürnberg: VTR, 2002), 20.

[46] Richebächer, "Missio Dei," 156–57, for that reason calls for an expansion of the expression "missio Dei triuni."

[47] Ibid, 145–48; see also Theo Sundermeier, "Missio Dei heute: Zur Identität christlicher Mission," Theologische Literaturzeitung 127, no. 12 (2002): 1243–44.

[48] Richebächer, "Missio Dei," 148–52.

Only against this backdrop can we understand why, ironically, the slogan *missio Dei* became a justification for the church's *not* having to conduct missions work. Richebächer explains:

> "It should not be made into the equivalent of the statement, 'God is the sole subject of missions,' which is what happened in the 1950s and 1960s. Such a one-sided definition is also not what stands behind the numerous, earlier statements by Hartenstein about God as the main actor in missions, which he had made since 1927 under the influence of Barth's theology. According to Karl Barth's lecture in 1932, it was even certain for Barth that the church was firmly established as the subject of missionary activity, something which can only be caused by God yet occurring within the basic event of encounter between humankind and the Word. It was in that lecture that he was the first to use the term 'mission' from the teaching on the 'opera Trinitatis' in a missiological-theological manner."[49]

---

[49] Ibid, 146.

2 Biblical-Systematic Section

An "Orthodox" Concept?

Is missio Dei, however, also a valid biblical concept compatible with the confessions of faith of the classical Christian churches? And is it also compatible with Reformed theology (as a Reformed theologian, one should grant me the privilege to address this question)? Indeed, the concept of missio Dei is valid and belongs to the heart of Christianity, regardless of whether it is used to indicate that God sent himself to redeem the world or that the mission of the church is the result of God's mission.

Missio Dei means no less than to recognize that sending (Greek: apostello and pempo and related words; Latin: missio, etc.) for redemption is the essence and center of the Christian faith. It is directly anchored in God and in his essence. Without the Trinity and without a God who sends himself, there would be no redemption. There would also be neither reason nor justification for the church's being sent to all peoples and for its sending missionaries everywhere. The term missio Dei was coined by St. Augustine and is thus traceable back to a man who is important not only for Catholic theology, but also for Luther and Calvin and their concept of the sending of Christ, as well as one who deeply influenced their biblical concept of grace. The main reason for the validity of missio Dei for Protestants is, however, the fact that it is firmly rooted in biblical revelation.

The genitive in *missio Dei* can, viewed grammatically, be seen as God being sent as well as God sending. Both aspects of missio Dei can be found in biblical texts, including those using terms for sending and those describing the relationship between the persons of the Trinity and the relationship between Jesus and his church. The church becomes part of God's sending.

Participation in God's actions and plans does not apply only to missio Dei. Rather, it is also applies to other central topics of Holy Scripture. Reformed theologians have correctly emphasized, for example, that believers and the church compose a part of the covenant that already exists between the Father and the Son. This was emphasized by one of the most important Reformed covenant theologians, Herman Witsius, in his major work in 1677. There is already within the Trinity a perfect, eternal covenant.[50] God's covenant with humankind is reception into the covenant of the Son with the Father: "And I confer[51] on you [via a covenant] a kingdom, just as my Father conferred [via a covenant] one on me" (Luke 22:29). The Father gave Jesus eternal rule and priesthood via a covenant (Hebrews 7:21–23; Galatians 3:17),[52] in which the church, as the body of Christ, receives an interest.

Reformed theologians in particular cherish the concept of the missio Dei, in particular because it emphasizes that redemption is always an act of God, even if God uses men and women as his ambassadors. Before God sent his people, he sent himself, and for that reason Jesus is the Lord of world missions. In addition to God's present and most recent sending of his people, God's sending of himself is also present, and for that reason the Holy Spirit is the seal and guarantee for world missions. Only the Holy Spirit can change the hearts of unbelievers. Human messengers are taken into God's plan, but a messenger cannot truly change any of his fellow humans to whom he or she speaks.

God's mission and God's covenant show that Christianity is a religion of salvation history and of historical advance. The different steps and aspects of missio Dei do not randomly follow each other and are not exchangeable. Rather, they follow God's wise design, according to which he unfolds his Kingdom step by step. *Missio Dei does not occur cyclically time and again. Rather, it points to the great goal of the entirety of history.*

Sending in the New Testament

In the New Testament, Jesus' sending of the disciples is viewed as the continuation of the sending of Jesus by his Father and the sending of the Spirit by the Father and the Son. The sending of Jesus by the Father (Matthew 10:40; Mark 9:37; Luke 9:48; 10:16; Acts 3:20, 26; approx. 50 times in John, see the following) and the sending of the Holy Spirit by the Father and Jesus (John 14:26; 15:26; Luke 24:29) is designated by the same words "to send," "sending," etc. (Greek: *apostello* and *pempo* and related words, Latin: *missio*, etc.) and by other common expressions, such as the sending of people by God.

---

[50] Herman Witsius, *The Economy of the Covenants between God and Men: Comprehending a Complete Body of Divinity*, vol. 1 (Escondido, CA: The den Dulk Christian Foundation; Phillipsburg, NJ: Presbyterian and Reformed, 1990), 165–92 (original 1677).
[51] A technical expression for concluding a covenant is present here, which many translations only poorly express.
[52] Comp. to the three last named texts, ibid., 166–167.

This applies especially to the Gospel of John.⁵³ The sending of the disciples is understood as a continuation of the sending of Jesus by his Father (among the many references in John, see initially John 3:17; 10:16; 17:18, 21, 23; 13:31) and the sending of the Holy Spirit by the Father and Jesus (John 14:26; 15:26). In John 8:42, Jesus says to his Father: "For I came from God and now am here. I have not come on my own; but he sent me."

It is surely no coincidence that Jesus, who sees himself as God's sent one, whereby the word *apostello* (to send) is frequently used, not only sends (*apostello*) his closest colleagues but also names them with the qualifying term of *apostle*.⁵⁴

Jesus, the Holy Spirit, and the Apostles as Sent by God:
Sending in the four Gospels
(A) = apostello; (P) = pempo (both roots are used interchangeably)

Jesus sent by the Father (Jesus speaking about himself)

Matthew 10:40: (A) "He who receives you receives me, and he who receives me receives the one who sent me."
Mark 9:37: (A) "Whoever welcomes one of these little children in my name welcomes me; and whoever welcomes me does not welcome me but the one who sent me."
Luke 4:18: (A) "The Spirit of the Lord is on me, because he has anointed me to preach good news to the poor. He has sent me to proclaim freedom for the prisoners and recovery of sight for the blind, to release the oppressed ..."
Luke 9:48: (A) "Then he said to them, 'Whoever welcomes this little child in my name welcomes me; and whoever welcomes me welcomes the one who sent me.'"
Luke 10:16: (A) "He who listens to you listens to me; he who rejects you rejects me; but he who rejects me rejects him who sent me."
John 3:17: (A) "For God did not send his Son into the world to condemn the world, but to save the world through him."

---

⁵³ On the significance of the sending of Jesus for mission in the Gospel of John, see Albert Curry Winn, *A Sense of Mission: Guidance from the Gospel of John* (Philadelphia: Westminster Press, 1981), 23, 30–34; W. F. Howard, *Christianity: According to St. John* (London: Duckworth, 1958), 25; Jose Comblin, *Sent from the Father: Meditations on the Fourth Gospel* (Maryknoll, NY: Orbis Books, 1981), 1–6.

⁵⁴ As mentioned, *pempo* can be used interchangeably.

John 4:34: (P) "'My food,' said Jesus, 'is to do the will of him who sent me and to finish his work.'"

John 5:23: (P) "... that all may honor the Son just as they honor the Father. He who does not honor the Son does not honor the Father, who sent him."

John 5:24: (P) "I tell you the truth, whoever hears my word and believes him who sent me has eternal life and will not be condemned; he has crossed over from death to life."

John 5:30: (P) "By myself I can do nothing; I judge only as I hear, and my judgment is just, for I seek not to please myself but him who sent me."

John 5:36: (A) "For the very work that the Father has given me to finish, and which I am doing, testifies that the Father has sent me."

John 5:37: (P) "And the Father who sent me has himself testified concerning me. You have never heard his voice nor seen his form ..."

John 5:38: (A) "... nor does his word dwell in you, for you do not believe the one he sent."

John 6:29: (A) "Jesus answered, 'The work of God is this: to believe in the one he has sent.'"

John 6:38: (P) "For I have come down from heaven not to do my will but to do the will of him who sent me."

John 6:39: (P) "And this is the will of him who sent me, that I shall lose none of all that he has given me, but raise them up at the last day."

John 6:44: (P) "No one can come to me unless the Father who sent me draws him, and I will raise him up at the last day."

John 6:57: (A) "Just as the living Father sent me and I live because of the Father, so the one who feeds on me will live because of me."

John 7:16: (P) "Jesus answered, 'My teaching is not my own. It comes from him who sent me.'"

John 7:18: (P) "He who speaks on his own does so to gain honor for himself, but he who works for the honor of the one who sent him is a man of truth; there is nothing false about him."

John 7:28: (P) "Yes, you know me, and you know where I am from. I am not here on my own, but he who sent me is true. You do not know him ..."

John 7:29: (A) "... but I know him because I am from him and he sent me."

John 7:33: (P) "I am with you for only a short time, and then I go to the one who sent me."

John 8:16: (P) "But if I do judge, my decisions are right, because I am not alone. I stand with the Father, who sent me."

John 8:18: (P) "I am one who testifies for myself; my other witness is the Father, who sent me."

John 8:26: (P) "I have much to say in judgment of you. But he who sent me is reliable, and what I have heard from him I tell the world."

John 8:29: (P) "The one who sent me is with me; he has not left me alone, for I always do what pleases him."

John 8:42: (A) "Jesus said to them, 'If God were your Father, you would love me, for I came from God and now am here. I have not come on my own; but he sent me.'"

John 9:4: (P) "As long as it is day, we must do the work of him who sent me. Night is coming, when no one can work."

John 10:36: (A) "... what about the one whom the Father set apart as his very own and sent into the world? Why then do you accuse me of blasphemy because I said, I am God's Son?"

John 11:42: (A) "I knew that you always hear me, but I said this for the benefit of the people standing here, that they may believe that you sent me."

John 12:44: (P) "Then Jesus cried out, 'When a man believes in me, he does not believe in me only, but in the one who sent me.'"

John 12:45: (P) "When he looks at me, he sees the one who sent me."

John 12:49: (P) "For I did not speak of my own accord, but the Father who sent me commanded me what to say and how to say it."

John 13:16: (P) "I tell you the truth, no servant is greater than his master, nor is a messenger greater than the one who sent him."

John 13:20: (P) "I tell you the truth, whoever accepts anyone I send accepts me; and whoever accepts me accepts the one who sent me."

John 14:24: (P) "He who does not love me will not obey my teaching. These words you hear are not my own; they belong to the Father who sent me."

John 15:21: (P) "They will treat you this way because of my name, for they do not know the One who sent me."

> John 16:5: (P) "Now I am going to him who sent me, yet none of you asks me, 'Where are you going?'"
>
> John 17:3: (A) "Now this is eternal life: that they may know you, the only true God, and Jesus Christ, whom you have sent."
>
> John 17:8: (A) "For I gave them the words you gave me and they accepted them. They knew with certainty that I came from you, and they believed that you sent me."
>
> John 17:18: (A) "As you sent me into the world, I have sent them into the world."
>
> John 17:21: (A) "that all of them may be one, Father, just as you are in me and I am in you. May they also be in us so that the world may believe that you have sent me."
>
> John 17:22-23: (A) "I have given them the glory that you gave me, that they may be one as we are one: I in them and you in me. May they be brought to complete unity to let the world know that you sent me and have loved them even as you have loved me."
>
> John 17:25: (A) "Righteous Father, though the world does not know you, I know you, and they know that you have sent me."
>
> John 20:21: (P) "Again Jesus said, 'Peace be with you! As the Father has sent me, I am sending you.'"

Jesus sent (Jesus speaking about himself without expressly naming the Sender)

> Matthew 15:24: (A) "He answered, 'I was sent only to the lost sheep of Israel.'"
>
> Luke 4:43: (A) "But he said, 'I must preach the good news of the kingdom of God to the other towns also, because that is why I was sent.'"

Jesus sent by the Father (stated by others than Jesus)

> Matthew 11:10, Mark 1:2, Luke 7:27: (A) "This is the one about whom it is written: 'I will send my messenger ahead of you, who will prepare your way before you.'"
>
> John 3:34-35: (A) [John the Baptist said,] "For the one whom God has sent speaks the words of God, for God gives the Spirit without limit. The Father loves the Son and has placed everything in his hands."

Acts 3:20: (A) "… and that he may send the Christ, who has been appointed for you - even Jesus."
Acts 3:26: (A) "When God raised up his servant, he sent him first to you to bless you by turning each of you from your wicked ways."
Acts 7:34: (A) (to Moses) "I have indeed seen the oppression of my people in Egypt. I have heard their groaning and have come down to set them free. Now come, I will send you back to Egypt."
Acts 7:35: (A) "This is the same Moses whom they had rejected with the words, 'Who made you ruler and judge?' He was sent to be their ruler and deliverer by God himself, through the angel who appeared to him in the bush."
Romans 8:3: (P) "For what the law was powerless to do in that it was weakened by the sinful nature, God did by sending his own Son in the likeness of sinful man to be a sin offering. And so he condemned sin in sinful man."
1 John 4:9: (A) "This is how God showed his love among us: He sent his one and only Son into the world that we might live through him."
1 John 4:10: (A) "This is love: not that we loved God, but that he loved us and sent his Son as an atoning sacrifice for our sins."
1 John 4:14: (A) "And we have seen and testify that the Father has sent his Son to be the Savior of the world."

Jesus sent by the Father (in one of Jesus' Parables)

Matthew 21:37: (A) "Last of all, he sent his son to them. 'They will respect my son,' he said."
Mark 12:6: (A) "He had one left to send, a son, whom he loved. He sent him last of all, saying, 'They will respect my son.'"
Luke 20:13: (P) "Then the owner of the vineyard said, 'What shall I do? I will send my son, whom I love; perhaps they will respect him.'"

The Holy Spirit sent by Jesus or by God the Father

Luke 24:49: (A) "I am going to send you what my Father has promised; but stay in the city until you have been clothed with power from on high."
John 14,26: (P) "But the Counselor, the Holy Spirit, whom the Father will send in my name, will teach you all things and will remind you of everything I have said to you."

John 15:26: (P) "When the Counselor comes, whom I will send to you from the Father, the Spirit of truth who goes out from the Father, he will testify about me."

John 16:7: (P) "But I tell you the truth: It is for your good that I am going away. Unless I go away, the Counselor will not come to you; but if I go, I will send him to you."

1 Peter 1:12: (A) "It was revealed to them that they were not serving themselves but you, when they spoke of the things that have now been told you by those who have preached the gospel to you by the Holy Spirit sent from heaven. Even angels long to look into these things."

Revelation 5:6: (A) "Then I saw a Lamb, looking as if it had been slain, standing in the center of the throne, encircled by the four living creatures and the elders. He had seven horns and seven eyes, which are the seven spirits of God sent out into all the earth."

Angels sent by God

Matthew 13:41: (A) "The Son of Man will send out his angels, and they will weed out of his kingdom everything that causes sin and all who do evil."

Matthew 24:31: (A) "And he will send his angels with a loud trumpet call, and they will gather his elect from the four winds, from one end of the heavens to the other."

Mark 13:27: (A) "And he will send his angels and gather his elect from the four winds, from the ends of the earth to the ends of the heavens."

Luke 1:19: (A) "The angel answered, 'I am Gabriel. I stand in the presence of God, and I have been sent to speak to you and to tell you this good news.'"

Luke 1:26: (A) "In the sixth month, God sent the angel Gabriel to Nazareth, a town in Galilee."

Hebrews 1:14: (A) "Are not all angels ministering spirits sent to serve those who will inherit salvation?"

Revelation 1:1: (A) "The revelation of Jesus Christ, which God gave him to show his servants what must soon take place. He made it known by sending his angel to his servant John."

Revelation 22:6: (A) "The Lord, the God of the spirits of the prophets, sent his angel to show his servants the things that must soon take place."

Revelation 22:16: (P) "I, Jesus, have sent my angel to give you this testimony for the churches. I am the Root and the Offspring of David, and the bright Morning Star."

The Word and, more specifically, salvation sent by God

Acts 10:36: (A) "You know the message God sent to the people of Israel, telling the good news of peace through Jesus Christ, who is Lord of all."

Acts 28:28: (A) "Therefore, I want you to know that God's salvation has been sent to the Gentiles, and they will listen!"

Jesus sends Apostles

Matthew 10:5: (A) "These twelve Jesus sent out with the following instructions ..."

Matthew 10:16a: (A) "I am sending you out like sheep among wolves."

Mark 3:14: (A) "He appointed twelve – designating them apostles – that they might be with him and that he might send them out to preach."

Mark 6:7: (A) "Calling the Twelve to him, he sent them out two by two and gave them authority over evil spirits."

Luke 9:2: (A) "... and he sent them out to preach the kingdom of God and to heal the sick."

Luke 10:1: (A) "After this the Lord appointed seventy-two others and sent them two by two ahead of him to every town and place where he was about to go."

Luke 10:3: (A) "Go! I am sending you out like lambs among wolves."

Luke 11:49: (A) "Because of this, God in his wisdom said, 'I will send them prophets and apostles, some of whom they will kill and others they will persecute.'"

Luke 22:35: (A) "Then Jesus asked them, 'When I sent you without purse, bag or sandals, did you lack anything?' 'Nothing,' they answered."

John 4:38: (A) "I sent you to reap what you have not worked for. Others have done the hard work, and you have reaped the benefits of their labor."

John 13:20: (P) "I tell you the truth, whoever accepts anyone I send accepts me; and whoever accepts me accepts the one who sent me."

John 17:18: (A) "As you sent me into the world, I have sent them into the world."

John 20:21: (P/A) "Again Jesus said, 'Peace be with you! As the Father has sent me, I am sending you.'"

Acts 9:17: (A) "Then Ananias went to the house and entered it. Placing his hands on Saul, he said, 'Brother Saul, the Lord – Jesus, who appeared to you on the road as you were coming here – has sent me so that you may see again and be filled with the Holy Spirit.'"

Acts 26:17: (A) (to Paul) "I will rescue you from your own people and from the Gentiles. I am sending you to them."

1 Corinthians 1:17: (A) "For Christ did not send me to baptize, but to preach the gospel – not with words of human wisdom, lest the cross of Christ be emptied of its power."

God sends people (in one of Jesus' parables)

Matthew 22:3: (A) "He sent his servants to those who had been invited to the banquet to tell them to come, but they refused to come."

Matthew 22:4: (A) "Then he sent some more servants and said, 'Tell those who have been invited that I have prepared my dinner: My oxen and fattened cattle have been butchered, and everything is ready. Come to the wedding banquet.'"

Luke 14:17: (A) "At the time of the banquet he sent his servant to tell those who had been invited, 'Come, for everything is now ready.'"

Prophets including John the Baptist

Matthew 23:34: (A) "Therefore I am sending you prophets and wise men and teachers. Some of them you will kill and crucify; others you will flog in your synagogues and pursue from town to town."

Matthew 23:34: (A) "O Jerusalem, Jerusalem, you who kill the prophets and stone those sent to you, how often I have longed to gather your children together, as a hen gathers her chicks under her wings, but you were not willing."

Luke 4:26: (P) "Yet Elijah was not sent to any of them, but to a widow in Zarephath in the region of Sidon."

> Luke 11:49: (A) "Because of this, God in his wisdom said, 'I will send them prophets and apostles, some of whom they will kill and others they will persecute.'"
>
> Luke 13:34: (A) "O Jerusalem, Jerusalem, you who kill the prophets and stone those sent to you, how often I have longed to gather your children together, as a hen gathers her chicks under her wings, but you were not willing!"
>
> John 1:6: (A) "There came a man who was sent from God; his name was John."
>
> John 1:33: (P) (John the Baptist) "I would not have known him, except that the one who sent me to baptize with water told me, 'The man on whom you see the Spirit come down and remain is he who will baptize with the Holy Spirit.'"
>
> John 3:28: (P) (John the Baptist) "You yourselves can testify that I said, 'I am not the Christ but am sent ahead of him.'"

People are sent by the church and by apostles

> Acts 8:14: (A) "When the apostles in Jerusalem heard that Samaria had accepted the word of God, they sent Peter and John to them."
>
> Acts 15:22: (P) "Then the apostles and elders, with the whole church, decided to choose some of their own men and send them to Antioch with Paul and Barnabas. They chose Judas (called Barsabbas) and Silas, two men who were leaders among the brothers."
>
> Acts 15:25: (P) "So we all agreed to choose some men and send them to you with our dear friends Barnabas and Paul."
>
> Acts 15:33: (A) "After spending some time there, they were sent off by the brothers with the blessing of peace to return to those who had sent them."
>
> Acts 19:22: (A) "He sent two of his helpers, Timothy and Erastus, to Macedonia, while he stayed in the province of Asia a little longer."
>
> Romans 10:15: (A) "And how can they preach unless they are sent? As it is written, 'How beautiful are the feet of those who bring good news!'"
>
> 1 Corinthians 4:17: (P) "For this reason I am sending to you Timothy, my son whom I love, who is faithful in the Lord. He will remind you of my way of life in Christ Jesus, which agrees with what I teach everywhere in every church."

1 Corinthians 16:3: (P) "Then, when I arrive, I will give letters of introduction to the men you approve and send them with your gift to Jerusalem."

2 Corinthians 9:3: (P) "But I am sending the brothers in order that our boasting about you in this matter should not prove hollow, but that you may be ready, as I said you would be."

2 Corinthians 12:17: (A) "Did I exploit you through any of the men I sent you?"

Ephesians 6:22 (P) "I am sending him to you for this very purpose, that you may know how we are, and that he may encourage you."

Philippians 2:19: (P) "I hope in the Lord Jesus to send Timothy to you soon, that I also may be cheered when I receive news about you."

Philippians 2:23: (P) "I hope, therefore, to send him as soon as I see how things go with me."

Philippians 2:25: (P) "But I think it is necessary to send back to you Epaphroditus, my brother, fellow worker and fellow soldier, who is also your messenger, whom you sent to take care of my needs."

Philippians 2:28: (P) "Therefore I am all the more eager to send him, so that when you see him again you may be glad and I may have less anxiety."

Colossians 4:8: (P) "I am sending him to you for the express purpose that you may know about our circumstances and that he may encourage your hearts."

1 Thessalonians 3:2: (P) "We sent Timothy, who is our brother and God's fellow worker in spreading the gospel of Christ, to strengthen and encourage you in your faith,"

1 Thessalonians 3:5: (P) "For this reason, when I could stand it no longer, I sent to find out about your faith. I was afraid that in some way the tempter might have tempted you and our efforts might have been useless."

2 Timothy 4:12: (A) "I sent Tychicus to Ephesus."

Titus 3:12: (P) "As soon as I send Artemas or Tychicus to you, do your best to come to me at Nicopolis, because I have decided to winter there."

2 Biblical-Systematic Section

The state sent by God

> 1 Peter 2:14: (P) "Submit yourselves ... whether to the king, as the supreme authority, or to governors, who are sent by him to punish those who do wrong and to commend those who do right."

Judgment sent by God

> 2 Thessalonians 2:11: (P) "For this reason God sends them a powerful delusion so that they will believe the lie ..."
>
> Revelation 14:15: (P) "Then another angel came out of the temple and called in a loud voice to him who was sitting on the cloud, 'Take your sickle and reap, because the time to reap has come, for the harvest of the earth is ripe.'"
>
> Revelation 14:18: (P) "Still another angel, who had charge of the fire, came from the altar and called in a loud voice to him who had the sharp sickle, 'Take your sharp sickle and gather the clusters of grapes from the earth's vine, because its grapes are ripe.'"

Jesus says in John 17:18, "As you sent me into the world, I have sent them into the world," and in John 20:21 he changes this into a personal address to his disciples: "As the Father has sent me, I am sending you." God the Father sends his Son and his Spirit as missionaries, and the church continues this sending mandate in world missions, whereby it remains dependent upon the exalted Lord (Matthew 28:18-20) and the Holy Spirit (Acts 1:8).

In the process, the high priestly prayer of John 17 is Jesus' announcement of consummation to his Father that he had conveyed God's Word to the disciples and had prepared them to carry the message into the world. If we examine the internal reasoning within the central passage regarding the missio Dei, it becomes clearer just how important a matter it is for Jesus and John that the entire world believe in Jesus Christ: "As you sent me into the world, I have sent them into the world. ... My prayer is not for them alone. I pray also for those who will believe in me through their message, that all of them may be one, Father, just as you are in me and I am in you. May they also be in us so that the world may believe that you have sent me. I have given them the glory that you gave me, that they may be one as we are one. ... May they be brought to complete unity to let the world know that you sent me and have loved them even as you have loved me" (John 17:18-23).

That Jesus also had a work to complete with respect to his disciples in addition to his work of redemption on the cross is shown through the entire high priestly prayer in John 17. In John 17:4, Jesus says to his Father, "I have brought you glory on earth by completing the work you gave me to do," and he adds by way of explanation: "Now they know that everything you have given me comes from you. For I gave them the words you gave me and they accepted them. They knew with certainty that I came from you, and they believed that you sent me" (John 17:7-8).

From the very beginning of the time of instruction, Jesus had in mind the goal of a close tie to him in the coming Great Commission (Matthew 28:18-20). For the time between Jesus' resurrection and his ascension, all the Gospel writers have handed down various forms of the Great Commission as a mandate for Jesus' disciples to conduct world missions (above all Matthew 28:16-20; Mark 16:15-20; John 20:11 - 21:24, esp. 20:21-23; Luke 24:13-53, esp. 24:44-49; Acts 1:4-11). It is no surprise that the great commission soon came to be known as Jesus' "command" (Acts 1:2; 10:42). In all the Gospels, however, this command is only the fulfilment of what was presaged with the selection of the disciples.

The Twelve Apostles had already listened to Jesus before their change of direction to discipleship with Jesus. Initially, then, all twelve were in a general sense disciples of Jesus. Only later were they chosen from the larger group of disciples to become apostles. (As examples of calling into general discipleship: John 1:35-42; Peter fishing, Luke 5:1-11; the calling of Levi (i.e., Matthew]), Matthew 9:9-13, Mark 2:13-17, Luke 5:27-32; see also the calling of the other disciples in Matthew 4:18-22, Mark 1:16-20).

All the Synoptic Gospels provide reports of the calling of the Twelve Apostles and, in the process, give a complete list of names (Matthew 10:1-4; Mark 3:13-17; Luke 6:12-16). Let us take a brief look at the three reports. "Jesus went up on a mountainside and called to him those he wanted, and they came to him. He appointed twelve - designating them apostles - that they might be with him and that he might send them out to preach and to have authority to drive out demons. These are the twelve he appointed: Simon (to whom he gave the name Peter); James son of Zebedee and his brother John (to them he gave the name Boanerges, which means Sons of Thunder); Andrew, Philip, Bartholomew, Matthew, Thomas, James son of Alphaeus, Thaddaeus, Simon the Zealot and Judas Iscariot, who betrayed him" (Mark 3:13-19). "He called his twelve disciples to him and gave them authority to drive out evil spirits and to heal every disease and sickness" (Matthew 10:1; the names of the Twelve follow in verses 2-4). "Jesus went out to a mountainside to pray, and spent the night praying to God" (Luke 6:12). Subsequently, he called his "disciples" to himself and "chose twelve of them, whom he also designated apostles" (Luke 6:13, with the names listed in 6:14-16). Jesus therefore had more followers who were not chosen as apostles. That there were other disciples in addition to the twelve disciples becomes clear on various occasions. Luke 6:17 differentiates between "a multitude of his disciples" and "a multitude of people."

To quote Mark again: "Jesus ... appointed twelve – designating them apostles – *that they might be with him and that he might send them out to preach* and to have authority to drive out demons. These are the twelve he appointed ..." (Mark 3:13-16). The intensive fellowship with and dependency upon Jesus had the goal of commissioning. The disciples were not to live forever in close fellowship with Jesus. Rather, they were eventually to continue Jesus' mandate independently. And it is not by chance that the twelve received the label of apostle, which not only describes their assignment. Rather, it was to describe the essence of the faith that they were to declare.

Who sends whom in the Bible?	Example
The Father sends the Son	Galatians 4:4
The Father sends the Spirit	Galatians 4:6
The Son sends the Spirit	John 15:26
The Son sends the church	John 17:18
The church sends its members	Romans 10:15

For a start, missio Dei means that God is always initially the missionary himself, before he commissions people. Moreover, God is not only the sender but, in many cases, also the sent one.

Missio Dei also means that this was not only so historically in the fall, or in the sending of Jesus, or in the sending of the Spirit. Rather, in the person of the Holy Spirit, God also remains the actual missionary and sent one today.

God, the First Missionary

Who was the first missionary? Who was the first one sent to speak about the fact that God will execute judgment but to speak even more about God's grace?

God himself was and is the first missionary. After the Fall, the history of humankind, which had just begun, seemed to be coming to an end.

However, God did not let it stop there. Rather, in his grace he himself came into the Garden of Eden (Genesis 3:8-9) to look for Adam and Eve and to ask: "Where are you?" (Genesis 3:9). He announced judgment and the coming redemption (Genesis 3:14-21).

Let us take a look at the events after the Fall (Genesis 3:1-7). Genesis 3:8-9 reports that God came into the Garden of Eden and called for the people there. God is the missionary who chases after people; the people do not come to God. Adam and Eve did not come to God and say: "We have obviously done something wrong. What are we to do from here?" They hid themselves. They were scared of God and wanted to avoid God. They knew exactly what had been said beforehand. God himself comes and pronounces judgment. That is always a part of mission. For if there were no judgment, we would not need to speak about grace and forgiveness. God announces judgment, but at the same time he announces grace. He announces in grace that humanity and the devil will not become inseparably intertwined. Rather, he says, "And I will put enmity between you and the woman, and between your offspring and hers" (Genesis 3:15). Thus, our world is indeed marked by sin, but humanity always perceives this sin and evil as an enemy. Who is gladdened when he reads the collection of evil things in the daily newspaper? We all know that something is going wrong. This understanding becomes very important when an individual comes to faith. Evil and the devil are not "married" to humankind in such a way that they cannot be divided. And who can break them apart from each other? In Genesis 3:15, it is announced that a human offspring will crush the head of the serpent. This became reality in Jesus Christ. God is the first missionary.

Excursus: Sending in the Old Testament

Francis M. DuBose has shown that the New Testament concept of mission is inherent in the Old Testament.[55] Sending, for instance, is included in the order to "go"[56] (Ezekiel 3:1; Amos 7:15, Jonah 1:2, 3:1; in the New Testament, e.g., Matthew 10:5-7; Luke 10:1-3; Matthew 28:19; Mark 16:15), whereby going is the consequence of sending (e.g., Jeremiah 1:7: "You must go to everyone I send you to"; Isaiah 6:8-9: "Send me! ... [to which God says] Go"; in the New Testament, see Acts 28:28). In Isaiah 55:11 God sends his Word, which "goes out" of his mouth: "So is my word that goes

---

[55] Francis M. DuBose, *God Who Sends: A Fresh Quest for Biblical Mission* (Nashville, TN: Broadman, 1983), 41-66.
[56] Ibid, 55-56.

out from my mouth: It will not return to me empty, but will accomplish what I desire and achieve the purpose for which I sent it." God also sends redemption (Psalm 111:9!; 110:2; Isaiah 19:20).

Just as in the Great Commission in the New Testament, in Isaiah 66:19 the saved ("those who survive") are sent: "I will set a sign among them, and I will send some of those who survive to the nations – to Tarshish, to the Libyans[b] and Lydians (famous as archers), to Tubal and Greece, and to the distant islands that have not heard of my fame or seen my glory. They will proclaim my glory among the nations."

Examples of Sending in the Old Testament

Moses (sometimes with Aaron) and the Exodus from Egypt: Exodus 3:10-15; 4:13-28; 5:22; 7:16; 33:12; Leviticus 16:28-29; 34:11; Joshua 24:5-6; 1 Samuel 12:8; Psalm 105:25-26; Psalm 135; Psalm 78; Micah 6:4
Joseph: Genesis 45:5-8; Psalm 105:17
Prophets in general: Judges 6:8; 2 Chronicles 36:15; Jeremiah 7:25; 25:4; 26:5; 29:19; 35:15; 44:4
Prophets mentioned by Name: Judges 6:14; 1 Samuel 12:11; 15:1; 16:1; 20:22; 2 Sam 12:1; 2 Kings 2; Isaiah 6:8; Jeremiah 42:6
The Messiah: Isaiah 61:1 ("The Spirit of the Sovereign Lord is on me"); Malachi 3:1; 3:23 (= 4:5)
The Angel of the Lord: Genesis 19:3; 24:7; 24:40; Exodus 23:20; Leviticus 20:16; 1 Chronicles 21:15; 2 Chronicles 7:13; Daniel 3:28; 6:22; Zechariah 1:10

Also important is DuBose's suggestion that God not only sends salvation and messengers of salvation, but also "sends" a message of judgment[57] (e.g., Exodus 8:21; 9:14; 15:7; Judges 9:23; 2 Kings 15:37; 24:2; 1 Chronicles 21:15; 32:21; Psalm 105:28; Isaiah 9:8; 10:6-16; Jeremiah 8:17; 9:16; 16:16; 23:38; 24:10; 25:15-17 and often in Jeremiah; Ezekiel 5:17; 14:19-21; 39:6; Hosea 8:14; Amos 1:4, 7, 10, 12; 2:2-5; 4:10; Malachi 2:2). In the New Testament one reads accordingly in 2 Thessalonians 2:11: "For this reason God sends them a powerful delusion so that they will believe the lie"; compare also Revelation 14:15-18 in which a sickle is "sent").

What God did here for the first time corresponded and corresponds so much to his being that it pervades all of history.

---

[57] Ibid, 60-66.

Jesus, the Missionary Par Excellence

Who for us is the missionary par excellence? It is not Paul, Boniface, or Hudson Taylor. The apostle and missionary par excellence, the "apostle and high priest" (Hebrews 3:1), is Jesus Christ. Why? He was sent by God to proclaim the gospel. Also, because Jesus was the Son of God, he not only declared the gospel but also, on the cross, he himself effected the gospel.

At the very beginning of Jesus' ministry, it is reported that he preached and evangelized (Matthew 4:17). "Jesus traveled about ... proclaiming the good news of the kingdom of God" (Luke 8:1). Jesus came for that reason. It was not enough for the gospel to be simply proclaimed, however; Jesus also had to accomplish it himself and bring about the needed atonement, reconciliation, and forgiveness.

Jesus is the missionary par excellence. Jesus was sent to earth by God, the Father, as a human being to take the penalty of the cross upon himself and to effect and proclaim salvation. God had already decided before the creation of the world (Ephesians 1:4) not to abandon people to their self-determined fate (John 3:16). Rather, he decided to send himself into the world in the form of Jesus as a missionary (John 3:16).

"The missionary movement, of which we are a part, has its origins in the Triune God. From the depths of his love to us, the Father sent his own beloved Son in order to reconcile all things with himself so that we and all people – through the Holy Spirit, might become one in him with the Father. ... In Christ we are ... ordained to full participation in his sending. One cannot share in Christ without sharing in his mission to the world. God's same acts, by which the church receives its existence, are those which obligate its global missions. Hartenstein summarizes this briefly in the following manner: 'The sending of the Son in order to reconcile the cosmos by the power of the Spirit is the origin and end of missions. From the 'missio Dei' alone comes the 'missio ecclesiae.' For this reason, mission is placed within the farthest reaching framework of God's salvation history and plan for salvation.'"[58]

---

[58] Richebächer, "Missio Dei," 145.

Jesus Receives Everything from His Father

Not His but God's Will

John 4:34: "'My food,' said Jesus, 'is to do the will of him who sent me and to finish his work.'"

John 5:30: "By myself I can do nothing; I judge only as I hear, and my judgment is just, for I seek not to please myself but him who sent me."

John 6:38: "For I have come down from heaven not to do my will but to do the will of him who sent me."

John 8:29: "The one who sent me is with me; he has not left me alone, for I always do what pleases him."

Not His Words but God's Words

John 7:16-17: "My teaching is not my own. It comes from him who sent me. If anyone chooses to do God's will, he will find out whether my teaching comes from God or whether I speak on my own."

John 8:28: "When you have lifted up the Son of Man, then you will know that I am [the one I claim to be] and that I do nothing on my own but speak just what the Father has taught me."

John 12:49: "For I did not speak of my own accord, but the Father who sent me commanded me what to say and how to say it."

John 14:24: "These words you hear are not my own; they belong to the Father who sent me."

John 17:8: "For I gave them the words you gave me and they accepted them. They knew with certainty that I came from you, and they believed that you sent me."

Jesus Shares What He Received from God

John 5:30: "By myself I can do nothing; I judge only as I hear, and my judgment is just, for I seek not to please myself but him who sent me."

John 8:26: "I have much to say in judgment of you. But he who sent me is reliable, and what I have heard from him I tell the world."

John 8:40: "As it is, you are determined to kill me, a man who has told you the truth that I heard from God. Abraham did not do such things."

> John 8:46-47: "Can any of you prove me guilty of sin? If I am telling the truth, why don't you believe me? He who belongs to God hears what God says."
>
> John 15:15: "Instead, I have called you friends, for everything that I learned from my Father I have made known to you."

Jesus Knows God

> John 7:28-29: "I am not here on my own, but he who sent me is true. You do not know him, but I know him because I am from him and he sent me."
>
> John 8:54-55: "My Father, whom you claim as your God ... Though you do not know him, I know him. If I said I did not, I would be a liar like you, but I do know him and keep his word."
>
> John 17:25: "Righteous Father, though the world does not know you, I know you, and they know that you have sent me."

Not His but God's Deeds

> John 5:36: "I have testimony weightier than that of John. For the very work that the Father has given me to finish, and which I am doing, testifies that the Father has sent me."
>
> John 9:4: "As long as it is day, we must do the work of him who sent me. Night is coming, when no one can work."
>
> John 5:17-19: "'My Father is always at his work to this very day, and I, too, am working.' For this reason the Jews tried all the harder to kill him; not only was he breaking the Sabbath, but he was even calling God his own Father, making himself equal with God. Jesus gave them this answer: 'I tell you the truth, the Son can do nothing by himself; he can do only what he sees his Father doing, because whatever the Father does the Son also does.'"

Jesus Has His Life from the Father

> John 6:57: "Just as the living Father sent me and I live because of the Father, so the one who feeds on me will live because of me."

The Holy Spirit as Missionary (John 16:5-14)

Jesus has left this world. With the Ascension, he returned to his Father. Who is then to become the missionary par excellence? The Holy Spirit! For sure, Jesus remains our paradigm as a missionary and rules the world (Matthew 28:18) and the church (Ephesians 1:22). However, who is the most successful missionary in history? Again, it is not Paul, Boniface, or Hudson Taylor; rather, it is the Holy Spirit.

Jesus said quite clearly whom he would send, because he can and will conduct missions better. I have chosen only one text from a group of similar texts about the coming of the Holy Spirit (John 7:39; 14:16-19; 14:26-28; 15:26-27; Acts 1:5-8). In John 16:5-7 we read: "Now I am going to him who sent me, yet none of you asks me, 'Where are you going?' Because I have said these things, you are filled with grief. But I tell you the truth: It is for your good that I am going away. Unless I go away, the Counselor will not come to you; but if I go, I will send him to you."

Jesus says expressly that it is "good" or "expedient" (John 16:7) that he goes to the Father and that the Holy Spirit comes in his place in order to convict the world of sin, judgment, and justice so that there might be salvation.

What enables Jesus' words about people becoming disciples (Matthew 28:19) to be fulfilled? Clearly it is the Holy Spirit, who was poured out upon Jesus' church at Pentecost in order for world mission to be set in motion and to guarantee its success (Luke 24:49; Acts 1:8). Jesus says about the Holy Spirit that: "he will convict the world" (John 16:8). Will he really do this? Or does Jesus have to visibly come back so that the world is convicted? World mission is sustained by the Holy Spirit, who brings about the Kingdom of God through this means. Jesus operates through the Holy Spirit and is ruling invisibly in world mission and in his church through the Spirit at the present time (Matthew 28:20).

According to John 16:5-15, it is also better for world mission that Jesus is invisibly present (see Matthew 28:20) while the Holy Spirit wins the world for the gospel than if Jesus were to reside at some place upon the earth.

According to this, a visible return of Jesus at the beginning of a 1,000-year reign would not make missionary work easier but more difficult. If there is a 1,000-year reign, and if at that time an overwhelming number of people and people groups come to faith, according to the words of Jesus, this can only be the consequence of a special working of the Holy Spirit. Since Jesus can effect everything he wants through the Holy Spirit, Jesus' effectiveness would not be heightened by his bodily presence. Another coming of Jesus to the earth in order to proclaim the gospel himself would not be progress with respect to salvation history. Rather, it would be a step backwards to a time prior to the pouring out of the Holy Spirit, thus a step into the time prior to New Testament world missions. According to Jesus' words (John 16:14), the Holy Spirit takes everything from what is Jesus' and proclaims nothing other than Jesus himself.

The Holy Spirit is apparently the better missionary for us and for worldwide outreach. Jesus himself said, "It is good for you." The disciples were sad. If they had thought only of themselves, they would have said, "What does this mean here, that the Holy Spirit is the better missionary? What could be better than to personally talk with Jesus?" However, Jesus did not just think about his twelve disciples. The whole time he was thinking about the entire world. For reaching the world through mission, the Holy Spirit – and I want to say this carefully – is better suited, or more "profitable," as Jesus himself says. It is expedient that he come because he can work not only in Jerusalem and in Israel, but throughout the entire world. "When he comes, he will convict the world of guilt in regard to sin and righteousness and judgment." For that reason, Jesus says to the woman at the well, "Believe me, woman, a time is coming when you will worship the Father neither on this mountain nor in Jerusalem. ... Yet a time is coming and has now come when the true worshipers will worship the Father in spirit and truth, for they are the kind of worshipers the Father seeks" (John 4:21, 23).

Who was thus the first missionary? God in the Garden of Eden. Who was the most important missionary? Jesus as God, whom the Father sent into the world in order to proclaim the gospel (John 3:16) and to accomplish it (1 John 2:2). *And who is the most successful missionary? God, the Holy Spirit.* For it is said of him that "he will convict the world of guilt in regard to sin and righteousness and judgment" (John 16:8).

Thus, it is not you or I, not Christians, and not the church but rather the Holy Spirit who will do this. The sending of Jesus' church is rooted in the fact that God initially sends himself (the Son and the Spirit) into the world as the first missionaries. The Spirit remains the missionary par excellence, and the church continues the Great Commission in the world. That is the reason for the existence of the New Testament church. The church is rooted in the Triune God himself and is unthinkable without God as both the sending one and the one sent.

As a result, the sending of the Spirit is bound to Jesus as it is to the Father. The Spirit is the Father's pledge to his Son: "Exalted to the right hand of God, he has received from the Father the promised Holy Spirit and has poured out what you now see and hear" (Acts 2:33).

The Holy Spirit glorifies the Father and the Son. Already in the Old Testament there is true praise of God by the Spirit (John 4:23-24), and Ephesians 5:18-19 links the fulfillment with the Spirit and with the praise and glorification of God through song and music. Following this, the Spirit glorifies Jesus (John 16:14) and proclaims only that which the Father instructs him to do (John 16:14-15). "I have much more to say to you, more than you can now bear. But when he, the Spirit of truth, comes, he will guide you into all truth. He will not speak on his own; he will speak only what he hears, and he will tell you what is yet to come. He will bring glory to me by taking from what is mine and making it known to you" (John 16:12-14). According to Jesus' words (John 16:14), the Holy Spirit only takes from Jesus and proclaims nothing other than Jesus himself.

When Jesus announced the coming of the Holy Spirit to his disciples, he mentioned the tasks of the Spirit: "When he comes, he will convict the world of guilt in regard to sin and righteousness and judgment" (John 16:8; see also verses 9-11). Wherever the Spirit of God is active, the cross of Calvary is not pushed into the background or degraded to a preliminary stage of belief; rather, we become aware that the holiness of God and the meaning of the atoning sacrifice of Christ in the place of the sinner overshadow everything.

EXCURSUS:
God Comes Near to Us –
on Differences between the Bible and the Koran

In the Christian faith, God comes close to humanity in his revelation. He comes to people, speaks with people in their language, and gives the relationship between God and humankind a sound basis. He does this by binding himself to his Word and by being absolutely faithful and reliable, and he thus enables faith and trust. For this very reason, the continuing revelation of God in the story of salvation is recorded in a written version, making the reliability more palpable and bringing God close to all individuals through human language.

The written revelation imposes its fulfillment in a manner in which God on his own *comes even closer* to us: God becomes man in Christ and "made his dwelling among us" (John 1:14). In Christ God becomes "Immanuel," "God with us" (Matthew 1:23). For that reason, the incarnation of God in Jesus does not repeal written revelation; rather, it fulfills and honors the true Word of God.

But that is not all! God wants to come still nearer to us. Jesus, true man and true God, leaves the earth with his new body and sends the Holy Spirit in his place, who can not only come much closer to all of humanity than Jesus but, since Pentecost even lives within all believers, God's Spirit testifying to their spirit and giving them the strength to live according to God's will (Romans 8:3-4). God cannot come any closer to us!

The Three Steps
Step 1: God comes close to humanity by speaking their language, revealing himself to them, and by delivering his will to them in written form. (e.g., 2 Timothy 3:14-17).
Step 2: God comes closer to humanity by becoming a human in Christ and by revealing himself directly to humankind (e.g., John 1:1, 14; 14:9).
Step 3: God comes closer still to humanity by dwelling through his Spirit in all those who believe in Jesus Christ. (e.g., Romans 8:9-14).

Since a Muslim can think only of God's Word as being without any human cooperation, it is very difficult for a Muslim to comprehend that the Bible is simultaneously a human word and the Word of God.[59]

It is even more difficult for a Muslim to comprehend that God and humanity come together in Jesus Christ, especially since a Muslim is shaped by the thought that this can be nothing other than idolatry.

However much this point stands in the center of the rejection of Christianity, since the Koran views Christians' great error as assigning the godhood of the one God to the human prophet Jesus, experience shows that the next step transcends a Muslim's powers of imagination, namely, that Christians believe that God's Spirit as the third person of the one God dwells in believers.

Pentecost: Missio Dei Par Excellence

Pentecost makes it clear that world mission in the power of the Spirit is the most important distinguishing mark of the church of Jesus Christ. At

---

[59] For more detail, see Thomas Schirrmacher, *The Koran and the Bible,* World of Theology, vol. 7 (Bonn: Culture and Science Publishing, 2013), online as a free download, http://www.bucer.org/resources/details/the-koran-and-the-bible.html

2 Biblical-Systematic Section

least twice Jesus told the disciples to wait until the Holy Spirit came before beginning the mission to all peoples (Mark 16:15-20; Acts 1:4-11). The Holy Spirit was to come in Jesus' place to convince the world of the gospel (John 16:7-11). When the Holy Spirit fell, the New Testament church and world missions began at the same time. On the day of Pentecost, the speaking in tongues and the miracle of each individual hearing what was said in his own language (those who were still Jewish and circumcised proselytes, respectively) made it clear to listeners from all parts of the Roman Empire that the gospel transcends all language and culture barriers through the power of the Holy Spirit.

Without the Holy Spirit, every attempt at world mission and every mission strategy would be condemned to fail. Only the Holy Spirit can convict humankind of their sin (John 16:7-10), lead them to the knowledge of God and Jesus' work of salvation, and make them new people in Christ (John 3:5). "We have not received the spirit of the world but the Spirit who is from God, that we may understand what God has freely given us. ... The man without the Spirit does not accept the things that come from the Spirit of God, for they are foolishness to him, and he cannot understand them, because they are spiritually discerned" (1 Corinthians 2:12, 14).

Even if God enlists Christians in world mission and would like them to use their reason in order to reach others (see, for example, Paul's many detailed travel plans and his general strategy in Romans chapters 1 and 15), all such mission strategies are tentative, because God alone decides whether they will lead to success (1 Corinthians 12:4-6; Romans 1:13).

The success of world mission as a result of the invisible lordship of Jesus Christ has been guaranteed by Jesus. In the Great Commission, Jesus justifies world mission by saying that he has "all authority in heaven and on earth" (Matthew 28:18) and that he is always with his church (Matthew 28:20). The Great Commission is thus not only a command but also a promise. Jesus himself will see to it that to "disciples of all nations" will happen (Matthew 28:19), for, as Jesus says, "I will build my church, and the gates of Hades will not overcome it" (Matthew 16:18). For that reason, John's revelation repeatedly announces that people from all languages and cultures will belong to an innumerable throng of the redeemed: "And they sang a new song: 'You are worthy to take the scroll and to open its seals, because you were slain, and with your blood you purchased men for God from every tribe and language and people and nation. You have made them to be a kingdom and priests to serve our God, and they will reign on the earth'" (Revelation 5:9-10; similarly Revelation 7:9; 10,11; 11:9; 13:7; 14:6; 17:15).

Acts 1:8 makes clear how missions should look: "But you will receive power when the Holy Spirit comes on you; and you will be my witnesses in Jerusalem, and in all Judea and Samaria, and to the ends of the earth." Who conducts world missions? Jesus (Matthew 16:18) and the Holy Spirit (Acts 1:8). Without the Spirit of God, this does not work. The Holy Spirit will convict the world. The Holy Spirit is the guarantee for missions. If Pentecost had not happened, there would be no world missions. However, Pentecost does not represent simply people becoming active, moving beyond their borders, and doing things that would otherwise not be possible. Rather, it shows that the Spirit of God has begun his work of world mission and that only through him can believers do the impossible, as all things are possible for God.

We are Enlisted – not in spite of but rather on account of the Holy Spirit

"He will convict the world," one reads above regarding the Holy Spirit (John 16:8). We often pose the question of predestination and responsibility and want to know how our responsibility is to be reconciled with God's ruling all things. However, the opposite question can also be asked: what do we have to do with missions if the Father, the Son, and the Holy Spirit do everything and if the Spirit convicts the world?

What am I do to as a witness? Can I bring someone else to faith? Or does God do that? To bring another person to faith, one needs the Holy Spirit. However, we cannot simply content ourselves with the fact that the Holy Spirit has the task of revealing the gospel to other people. Whoever has received the power of the Holy Spirit, which is the precondition for even being able to proclaim the gospel at all, does not remain quiet in his easy chair. Rather, he becomes a witness.

It is not the case that the church of Jesus Christ has a "missions program" and now has to consider what role God will play in it. It is also not the case that we need God as the command device, so that we can say to critics, "We have the order directly from God." That would be far too little. It is not as if God has given us only an order to conduct missions. There is a promise standing behind the order, and in the final event is it the missio Dei or the being of God himself.

Our task of conducting missions is a direct continuation of God's mission. For that reason, it is a decisive question to ask why God includes us in mission when he could get along just as well (or perhaps far more easily) alone. The Holy Spirit wishes to convict people of sin. For that reason, it would seem, it is nonsense to employ us for this purpose!

The astonishing thing about the Great Commission is not the Holy Spirit's participation, but our participation! Stated alternatively, why is there a Great Commission anyway? If in the Garden of Eden and repeatedly throughout history God pursues people, why does he still commission people? If Jesus is the missionary par excellence, to whom we owe thanks for our faith – and according to the book of Hebrews, Jesus is the apostle (Hebrews 3:1) – why are people still needed? If above all things the Holy Spirit has one task ("he will convict the world of guilt in regard to sin and righteousness and judgment"), what do we have to do with that? That is, in my opinion, the real question.

John Calvin rightly wrote, "God might have acted, in this respect, by himself, without any aid or instrument, or might even have done it by angels; but there are several reasons why he chooses to employ men."[60] As the first reason, Calvin mentions God's regard for people as his own creation and image.

A modern Reformed theologian, John Stott, writes similarly: "The place which the Holy Spirit has in evangelization is primary. This is due to the fact that the Holy Spirit is himself the chief evangelist, the main witness, and the first communicator of the gospel. Normally, he does not evangelize without the aid of human tools. And yet, without the aid of the Holy Spirit, the work of human evangelists would in any case be fruitless."[61]

One has the Great Commission with the Holy Spirit himself as the missionary: missio Dei. However, the Holy Spirit sends us. We should recall at this point that when the Father in heaven sent his Son, he did not retire; it was his mission that Jesus conducted. Similarly, when Jesus sent the Holy Spirit, the Father and Jesus did not retire. Rather, Jesus rules at the right hand of God and says: "And surely I am with you always, to the very end of the age" (Matthew 28:20). When the Holy Spirit comes and charges Christians with proclaiming the gospel in all the world, he also does not retire. The Father *and* the Son *and* the Holy Spirit continue to

---

[60] John Calvin, *The Institutes of the Christian Religion*, (Grand Rapids, MI: Christian Classics Ethereal Library, 2002), 648-649, (Book 4, Chapter 3, Section 1). This is a modern reprint of the Beveridge English translation of the 1559 version of Calvin's important book. Online at: http://www.ntslibrary.com/PDF%20Books/Cal vin%20Institutes%20of%20Christian%20Religion.pdf

[61] John R. W. Stott, *Der Heilige Geist in der Evangelisation* (Denkendorf: Gnadauer Verlag, 1976), 12.

have *their* mission throughout the entire world, even if we are the ones who, in a manner of speaking, carry it out.

For that reason, the Great Commission aims at "baptizing them in the name of the Father and of the Son and of the Holy Spirit" (Matthew 28:19), whereby the singular of the name of the three persons of the Godhead is a classic reference to the divine Trinity of God. Since we are his image, God includes us fully in the task of missions, as individuals reconciled to him.

And everything that we people can do with our God-given abilities is used by God. There is only one thing which he does not request of us, and that is to do things that we cannot do, such as to look into the heart of others. However, as we have been made in the image of God, God has given us many abilities to employ, such as the ability to think about who our listeners really are (1 Corinthians 9:19–21). As normal people we are able to consider and observe what other people are thinking and who they are. And together, the global church is able to think about where its engagement is most urgent. However, God never thought that the entire program that stands behind the Great Commission would be something which we could autonomously implement. World mission is so gigantic that without God it cannot function at all. We are simply not in the position to do this. Only God, who according to his very nature is a missionary, can do this.

Typical examples in the Book of Acts are the conversion of the Roman centurion Cornelius (Acts 10:1–11, 18) and the finance minister of Ethiopia (Acts 8:26–40). In both cases, God indeed used massive miracles and dreams, but not to directly convert pagans. Rather, they were to bring people together with others who could tell them the gospel.

For instance, Anna Marie Aagaard has correctly linked the gifts of the Spirit closely to the founding and growth of the church with the sending of the Holy Spirit and missio Dei.[62] The gifts of the Spirit are an apparent demonstration that the missio Dei has not condemned humanity to passivity. On the contrary, God himself has enabled humankind to actively participate in the missio Dei. It is too bad that this topic has not long ago been leveraged by Evangelical theologians and missiologists.[63]

---

[62] Anna Marie Aagaard, "Missiones Die," in *Das Evangelium und die Zweideutigkeit der Kirche: Evangelium und Geschichte*, ed. Vilmos Vajta, vol. 3 (Vandenhoeck & Ruprecht, 1973), 97–112.

[63] See the discussion of spiritual gifts in Thomas Schirrmacher, *Ethik*, vol. 3 (Nürnberg: VTR; Hamburg: RVB, 2002), 77–90.

The gifts of the Spirit are also a good example of missio Dei and the complementarity of mission that God himself carries out and in which he fully includes people. God himself determines who has which gifts and tasks in the church and in mission. Nevertheless, the individual Christian and the church as a whole are not incapacitated by this. Rather, the Spirit enables Christians to introduce their special characteristics and individuality a fortiori.

The Unsuited Individual

God wishes to convict people of their sin and free them from the power of sin through atonement and forgiveness. How can he use sinful people like us? We know that many people – justifiably – have doubts about the church of Christ because Christians throughout history have committed many errors and sins. The Bible itself describes very critically the errors of God's people throughout history. Why is the church indispensable for the fulfillment of his plan of salvation and his mission, especially when it is never truly pure and unflawed?

How, for example, could God ever think of sending someone like Jonah as a missionary? He indeed knew beforehand how Jonah would react and how he thought in his heart. In sending Jonah, God sent someone to Nineveh who was not in agreement with his approach, after having stirred him to do so through much effort. By the way, Jonah was a good Jewish theologian. Why? Because he knew precisely that God wanted to be gracious not only to Israel but also to pagans. The reason for Jonah's anger resided precisely in this fact: "O Lord, is this not what I said when I was still at home? That is why I was so quick to flee to Tarshish. I knew that you are a gracious and compassionate God, slow to anger and abounding in love, a God who relents from sending calamity" (Jonah 4:2). Here it becomes clear that that *it was due to theological reasons and not due to personal reasons that Jonah fled from the Great Commission!* This Jewish prophet did not want the same rules to apply to pagans as to Jews. Who would voluntarily use someone like this? God could have saved himself a lot of work. Up to the present day, God has expended a lot of work moving believers in the direction of missions. Why did God not just speak from heaven himself to the inhabitants of Nineveh?

Another example of an unwilling missionary with theological concerns is Peter in his relationship to Cornelius. Peter had personally heard the missionary command, "Therefore go and make disciples of all nations" (Matthew 28:19). It was stated unequivocally that not only Jews were to hear the gospel. Then came Pentecost, in which Peter played a central role as all kinds of people came to faith, yet Peter still did not comprehend that the gospel was to go to all people. He still had problems with the fact that pagans could be saved without becoming Jews beforehand. On the other hand, there was Cornelius. Why did God send a dream to Cornelius without declaring in the dream how one could be converted? Instead, Cornelius is told only that Peter would come, and Peter was not at all ready to do so. So God sent another dream to Peter and declared to him that pagans were able to be saved and then sent him to Cornelius. What an effort? Why all of that? Only so that Cornelius could hear the gospel from Peter! Obviously, God did not send Peter because he was so terrific and indispensable.

It was not the case that Peter knew long before the crucifixion where things were headed, was always more eager than others, and said, "We want to see if we can reach the entire world." Rather, he was among those who had their doubts about Jesus and despaired. He heard the Great Commission and could not do anything with it. He not only experienced Pentecost but was the primary speaker there, and yet he did not grasp the most decisive thing, which was that the Holy Spirit was seeking people from all over the world: "He will convict the world." If the Holy Spirit wishes to speak to each heart, he can speak every language in the world. Peter experienced that. Nevertheless, months later God had to show Peter again that the Holy Spirit seeks to draw people from all ethnic groups into the church. Not until he experienced Cornelius's conversion did he finally understand what was at issue: "As I began to speak, the Holy Spirit came on them as he had come on us at the beginning" (Acts 11:15). He then testified to that at the apostolic council (Acts 15:7-11). He had finally understood that God does not differentiate among peoples.

Let us take a closer look at the shortcomings of the Old and New Testament missionaries using the example of the Great Commission according to Matthew (28:18-20). We generally read the text beginning at verse 18. However, what does the previous verse say? Jesus meets with his disciples, "but some doubted" (Matthew 28:17). That is the setting of the Great Commission! This is not the type of people with whom one begins a worldwide program! We probably would have said something like: "We have to work on this. And once you have gotten over your doubts, then we can talk about how you can slowly be introduced to bigger tasks." God's mission to the entire world rested on these doubters! Jesus assured them that "you will receive power when the Holy Spirit comes on you; and you will be my witnesses in Jerusalem, and in all Judea and Samaria, and to the ends of the earth" (Acts 1:8). Again, we can see that the disciples did not become witnesses because they were outstanding people; rather, they were fitting witnesses because they received the power of the Holy Spirit.

And how do we know that? As long as they did not have this power, they were prohibited from becoming missionaries. Jesus said to them – if I may put it in my own words: "Please just stay out of trouble in Jerusalem until the Holy Spirit comes! As long as the Holy Spirit has not come, you do not have the Great Commission and would also not even be in a position to carry it out!" It could not be clearer: only after the Holy Spirit has come does Jesus send out his disciples. Jesus tells his disciples, and he effectively tells us: "Never forget, without the Holy Spirit you cannot do anything. You can get a lot of public attention. You can get to the point where everyone talks about you. However, for anyone to be convinced in the deepest recesses of their heart, let alone for entire peoples to become disciples, takes something that only the Holy Spirit can do!"

Why in the world does God always want to have us involved with him when he conducts missions? Why does he give the Great Commission to people? I don't know. I know only one thing: That's the way it is! I also know that it is not our task to think about whether we would do it in exactly the same way if we were God. Whoever comes to believe in God and becomes a Christian receives the power of the Holy Spirit so as to be a witness. Mission is not only a command; rather, to begin with, it is simply a fact. An individual in whom the Holy Spirit truly lives cannot do anything other than to talk about salvation in Jesus Christ. What did Jesus proclaim? "He will bring glory to me" (John 16:14). Jesus wishes to make the Holy Spirit glorified in us and also in others.

So, to repeat, the passage prior to the Great Commission notes that "some doubted" (Matthew 28:17). And then the command comes: "Therefore go!" Proclaim the gospel, make disciples, and baptize them in the name of the Father and the Son and the Holy Spirit. And teach them to obey everything I have commanded you. That is a huge agenda. It is the most comprehensive agenda that people have ever received. Is it not evident that we people have been asked? That is now indeed something for us to go and do, is it not?

But what about the doubts beforehand? Humanly seen, the disciples were entirely useless for this task. We all know that the Great Commission is not complete if we understand it as a command. It is first of all a promise and an authorization. Without the first and last sentences, the Great Commission is empty chatter. But those sentences promise, "All authority in heaven and on earth has been given to me," and "Surely I am with you always, to the very end of the age" (Matthew 28:18, 20).

There is a peculiar tension between the disciples' doubts and the enormous task, which requires a lot of human sweat but is also not achievable without God. This tension makes sense only if the disciples are indeed stretched but if the mission is not dependent upon their performance. Rather, it depends upon the proxy given by the risen Lord and his presence through the Holy Spirit. We have to go. We have to proclaim. "Make disciples" is somewhat clumsy in German: *Machet zu Jüngern*. It means to see to it that people become disciples, that they become pupils, that they learn from God.

"Baptize them"? Why does the Holy Spirit not baptize people himself? That is precisely what he does! After all, baptism by water is only an external expression of the actual baptism by the Spirit (e.g., Acts 11:16). Nevertheless, Jesus wants every individual who comes to faith to have another person alongside who already belongs to God and who baptizes the individual when he publicly states that he belongs to God. Why is that? What does the person who comes to faith have to do with the person who baptizes him? Actually, nothing. The decisive thing is that baptism occurs in the name of the Father and the Son and the Holy Spirit. This fact means that the individual performing the baptism acts on behalf of God and that otherwise the divinely desired baptism is not possible.

For a reason known only to God, God desires that there be at least one other person there who already believes. Naturally, it is better if there are more witnesses. God has so desired that the gospel move from individual to individual and that we tell others, convince others, teach others, baptize others, and bring others into the church. God, who alone is Lord and good without us (Matthew 28:18–19), still does not want to build his kingdom without us.

Many biblical teachings can only be described in a complementary manner if we want to do justice to the totality of the Scriptures (*tota scriptura*). Complementarity means[64] that two or more facts can be delved into separately, documented, and described and can appear to be simultaneously true without our having an explanation for this situation. The central teachings of early Christian councils are all complementarian declarations, and only in that way were they able to do justice to the entirety of the Scriptures and produce enduring theological peace. Jesus is true man and true God, without confusion and without separation. God is one

---

[64] See Thomas Schirrmacher, *The Complementary Nature of Biblical Teaching*, MBS Text 29 (Bonn: Martin Bucer Seminar, 2004), available at http://www.bucer.org/resources/details/mbs-texte-029-2004-the-complementary-nature-of-biblical-teaching.html

and yet Father, Son, and Holy Spirit. In addition, on many other topics such as predestination and human responsibility, belief and knowledge, law and grace, love and the anger of God, teaching and life, the Holy Scriptures as one hundred percent a human word and one hundred percent a divine word, are classic examples of biblical complementarity.[65]

Belief Comes through Preaching: Romans 10:14–17

God accomplishes the proclamation of the message of salvation in Christ, which is solely caused and effected by God, in a manner whereby any sending is indeed authorized by him alone. However, the proclamation takes place through the concrete sending of people by people, and the changing of people's ways is achieved through the preaching of people who are sent. Paul formulates this understanding in Romans 10:14–16:

> "How, then, can they call on the one they have not believed in? And how can they believe in the one of whom they have not heard? And how can they hear without someone preaching to them? And how can they preach unless they are sent? As it is written [Isaiah 52:7], 'How beautiful are the feet of those who bring good news!' But not all the Israelites accepted the good news. For Isaiah says [Isaiah 53:1], 'Lord, who has believed our message?' Consequently, faith comes from hearing the message, and the message is heard through the word of Christ."

In Romans 10:14–15 Paul formulates a list which has become important for the history of missions far beyond the context of the text.[66] For someone to call upon God, belief is necessary. To believe, one must hear. For hearing to occur, "preaching" must take place (this word often sounds as if it is too limited to Sunday worship services). And for proclamation to take place, sending has to occur. This can be illustrated in the following manner:

(God) ⇔ Sending ⇔ Preaching ⇔ Hearing ⇔ Believing ⇔ Calling ⇔ God

---

[65] See Thomas Schirrmacher, "Bibeltreu oder der Bibel treu? Glaubwürdigkeit und Irrtumslosigkeit der Schrift," in *Wahrheit und Erfahrung: Themenbuch zur Systematischen Theologie*, vol. 1, ed. Christian Herrmann (Wuppertal: R. Brockhaus, 2004), 45–58.

[66] See A. F. Walls, "The First Chapter of the Epistle to the Romans and the Modern Missionary Movement," in *Apostolic History and the Gospel: Biblical and Historical Essays Presented to F. F. Bruce on his 60th Birthday*, ed. W. Ward Gasque and Ralph P. Martin (Grand Rapids, MI: Eerdmans, 1970), 346–57.

If one takes all of Romans 10:12-17 into consideration, this illustration can be expanded:

God ⇔ Word of Christ ⇔ Sending ⇔
⇔ Preaching ⇔ Hearing ⇔ Believing ⇔ Obeying ⇔
⇔ Calling ⇔ Confessing Christ ⇔ God

It is of central importance that God does not normally conduct missions directly through angels or by speaking directly to people. Rather, he sends people or, more specifically, he has them sent by the church, and they then pass on the gospel.

It is just as important that the gospel be passed on by proclamation and preaching and not via other avenues. Real evangelism does not occur through pictures without any commentary, or through feelings or instrumental music, to mention a few things as examples which are surely not forbidden and can absolutely be found within the framework of evangelism. However, they do not carry out the actual relaying of the message. "Consequently, faith comes from hearing the message, and the message is heard through the word of Christ" (Romans 10:17). What an inconceivable authority God gives to our speaking, that through this means alone his kingdom is expanded! For that very reason, however, Christians must be sure that they are truly going about doing God's work and not circulating their own ideas, cultural characteristics, or their own habitual bad behavior in the name of God.

Love and Missio Dei

Henning Wrogemann[67] and Theo Sundermeier[68] have both derived missio Dei from the love of God – in my opinion a central assertion which is much too little emphasized. "God comes to people as a lover."[69] For both these authors, embedding missio Dei in love brings about the creature's freedom to reject God and, with that, the need for mission efforts to respect this freedom in a non-coercive manner. "Mission efforts respect the freedom of the other individual,"[70] and we should continue missions in

---

[67] Wrogemann, "Gott ist Liebe," 301–2.
[68] Sundermeier, "Missio Dei heute," 1247; see also Theo Sundermeier. "Missio Dei: Zur Identität christlicher Mission," *Entwurf* (Fachgemeinschaft Ev. Religionslehrer in Württemberg, etc.), March 2003: 3–9.
[69] Sundermeier, "Missio Dei heute," 1247.
[70] Ibid; see also Wrogemann, "Gott ist Liebe," 302–4.

this way. Wrogemann argues for the expression "missio amoris Dei"[71] and advocates understanding this action on God's part as an expression not of his will but rather of his essence. As justifiable as it may be to embed missio Dei in the essence of God, it will not be helpful to set the essence and the will of God over against each other, for it is the essence of the love of God that it be expressed in action.

A clear example for embedding missions in the essence of God is the embedded nature of love in the Triune nature of God. There must at least be two persons for love to exist; that is, there is always a counterpart.[72] For that reason, a non-triune God can thus love only when he has created a counterpart.[73] Therefore, post-biblical Judaism, Islam, and other monotheistic religions have difficulty describing love as an eternal essential characteristic of God present before the Creation. The Triune God of the Bible, however, has the counterpart for love in himself. John 17:24 describes the Father's love for the Son prior to the creation of the world: "Father, I want those you have given me to be with me where I am, and to see my glory, the glory you have given me because you loved me before the creation of the world." Therefore, the eternal, intra-Trinitarian love is the epitome of love and the point of departure for all Christian love and ethics. The persons of the Trinity speak with each other, plan with each other, obey each other, act for each other, care for each other, honor each other, etc., and all these actions are related to love. When a person can function as created in the image of God, and to think, plan, act, and care for others, then all these characteristics and abilities are likewise also oriented toward love from the very beginning.

In the Bible, everything that is good comes from the Trinity. In Christianity, everything is rooted in the Trinity. The center of salvation history is that God sends himself to the earth and that Jesus himself sends his

---

[71] Wrogemann, "Gott ist Liebe," 302.

[72] Dennis Ngien, "Richard of St. Victor's Condilectus: The Spirit as Co-beloved," *European Journal of Theology* 12, no. 2 (2003): 77–92, refers to Richard of St. Viktor (ca. 1172), who took up this very thesis from St. Augustine in his principal work on the Trinity, *De Trinitate*, stating that love cannot be present where there is only one person.

[73] For more detail, see Thomas Schirrmacher, "Der trinitarische Gottesglaube und die monotheistischen Religionen," in *Die Einzigartigkeit Jesu Christi*, ed. Rolf Hille and Eberhard Troeger (Brockhaus: Wuppertal, 1993), 113–51; Thomas Schirrmacher, "Trinity in the Old Testament and Dialogue with the Jews and Muslims," *Calvinism Today* (now *Christianity and Society*) 1, no. 1 (January 1991): 21–27, reprinted as "Trinity in the Old Testament and Dialogue with Jews and Muslims," *Field Update: GR International* (April–May 1991): 6-8 and (June–July 1991): 5–8.

church into the world, while the Holy Spirit is sent simultaneously by the Father and the Son to be the executor of world missions. The Trinity has existed from all eternity, before the world existed. For that reason, loving, speaking, helping, listening, freedom, and obedience have existed since eternity. God does not require people in order to exist or in order to be good.

Because the members of the Trinity speak with each other and Jesus is the Word, we can speak with each other. Because the persons in the Trinity do not live only for themselves but rather for each other, humankind can be asked to do the same. Because the persons in the Trinity discuss and plan with each other, it is a biblical principle to not decide things on one's own.

Within the Trinity there is obedience, such as by the Son toward the Father. This occurs without someone being forced to do so. Everyone acts of his own accord. Love and law are identical. Jesus and his Father are completely alike as God, and for that reason, Jesus is boundlessly free and can at the same time obey the Father in what is to be executed in salvation history. Communication, love, honoring each other, and working for a goal outside ourselves – all that stems from the Trinity.

Jesus acts of his own accord and is obedient (both at the same time)

Philippians 2:8: "He humbled himself and became obedient to death – even death on a cross!"

John 10:11, 17-18: "I am the good shepherd. The good shepherd lays down his life for the sheep. ... The reason my Father loves me is that I lay down my life – only to take it up again. No one takes it from me, but I lay it down of my own accord. I have authority to lay it down and authority to take it up again. This command I received from my Father."

Jesus acts of his own accord

Hebrews 9:14: "How much more, then, will the blood of Christ, who through the eternal Spirit offered himself unblemished to God. ..."

Jesus obeys

Luke 22:42: "Father, if you are willing, take this cup from me; yet not my will, but yours be done."

> John 5:19: "Jesus gave them this answer: 'I tell you the truth, the Son can do nothing by himself; he can do only what he sees his Father doing, because whatever the Father does the Son also does.'"
>
> John 5:30–32: "By myself I can do nothing; I judge only as I hear, and my judgment is just, for I seek not to please myself but him who sent me. If I testify about myself, my testimony is not valid. There is another who testifies in my favor, and I know that his testimony about me is valid."
>
> John 8:28–29: "So Jesus said, 'When you have lifted up the Son of Man, then you will know that I am [the one I claim to be] and that I do nothing on my own but speak just what the Father has taught me. The one who sent me is with me; he has not left me alone, for I always do what pleases him.'"
>
> John 8:42: "... for I came from God and now am here. I have not come on my own; but he sent me."
>
> John 12:49–50: "For I did not speak of my own accord, but the Father who sent me commanded me what to say and how to say it. I know that his command leads to eternal life. So whatever I say is just what the Father has told me to say."
>
> Hebrews 5:8: "Although he was a son, he learned obedience from what he suffered."
>
> See also the additional texts discussed above from the Gospels, in which Jesus sees himself as the one sent by the Father.

Islam and post-biblical Judaism believe in a single God who, for want of a counterpart prior to the creation of the world, was not able to love anyone. Love is for that reason not rooted in the eternal essence of God; rather, at the earliest, love is conceivable from the time of creation. The Triune God of the Old and New Testament, on the other hand, was already love, without needing the creation for it. This is because he is three and one at the same time and can thus in himself love the respective other from all eternity. Without the Trinity, Christianity would no longer be the religion of love. For that reason, Karl Bernhard Hundeshagen wrote in 1853 what Christianity contributed to the question of human rights: "It is the immeasurable cultural significance of the Christian teaching of the Trinity of God in which the prerequisites are given to fully realize the conception of humanity."[74]

---

[74] Karl Bernhard Hundeshagen, *Ueber die Natur und geschichtliche Entwicklung der Humanitätsidee in ihrem Verhältnis zu Kirche und Staat* (Berlin: Verlag von Wiegen

EXCURSUS:
The Dual Concept of the Apostle in the New Testament

In Romans 15:15, Paul traces his office of apostleship back to "the grace God gave." That a spiritual gift (a gift of grace) can be designated by the word "grace" becomes clear in Romans 12:3–8. In Romans 15:15, "grace" designates Paul's call to be an apostle (see Romans 1:1), which gives him the right and the duty to teach other Christians with authority, as he does through the letter to the Romans. For Paul, his apostolic office was above all a service "to the Gentiles" (Romans 15:16). God called him in his conversion to preach to the non-Jews. Other apostles had also agreed with Paul that they, especially Peter, should be apostles to the "circumcised" or, more specifically, the "Jews." Paul, however, was to be an apostle to the "uncircumcised," thus meaning the Gentiles (Galatians 2:6–9). The other apostles, Paul writes, "recognized the grace given to me" (Galatians 2:9).

God accredited Paul for this apostolic office "by the power of signs and miracles, through the power of the Spirit" (Romans 15:19). In 2 Corinthians 12:12 one reads accordingly, "The things that mark an apostle – signs, wonders and miracles – were done among you with great perseverance." It is thus not a matter of signs and wonders in general but rather a matter of those that confirm the first witnesses of the gospel, as is clearly expressed in Hebrews 2:3–4: "This salvation, which was first announced by the Lord, was confirmed to us by those who heard him. God also testified to it by signs, wonders and various miracles, and gifts of the Holy Spirit distributed according to his will."

When Paul describes his missionary work in Romans 15 and the fact that he does not wish to proclaim the gospel where apostles have already been active and churches exist (Romans 15:19–21, 23), the question arises as to whether we can carry over his particular mandate as an apostle to our time. Are there still apostles today to whom what was said about Paul applies in a corresponding manner? Some say yes, while others say no. I believe that in a certain sense both sides are right, as we discover when we look at the New Testament evidence of who was called an apostle.

---

und Grieben, 1853), 29; see also the critical evaluation of this quotation in Theodor Christlieb, "Carl Bernhard Hundeshagen: Eine Lebensskizze," *Deutsche Blätter* (1873): 698.

On the basis of the following compilation of New Testament passages, I believe that today there are no longer apostles like Paul or Peter (Jesus Christ's apostles) whom God fully confirmed through signs and wonders and whose instruction was binding for the church.[75] However, the gift of grace and the office of apostle continue in a general sense ("apostles of the churches"). These apostles sent out by the church were and are missionaries who have the special gift of proclaiming the gospel in areas where there are still no Christians and no churches.

All Documented Evidence of the Word *Apostle* and the Term *Apostolic Ministry* (Point 9 Below) in the New Testament

1. Apostle = Jesus in the Letter to the Hebrews

Hebrews 3:1: "Fix your thoughts on Jesus, the apostle and high priest whom we confess."

2. Apostle = the 12 Apostles in the Gospels

Matthew 10:2; Mark 3:14; 6:30; Luke 9:10; 17:5; 22:14; 24:10

3. Apostle = apostles generally in the Gospels

Luke 11:49: "Because of this, God in his wisdom said, 'I will send them prophets and apostles, some of whom they will kill and others they will persecute.'"
John 13:16: "I tell you the truth, no servant is greater than his master, nor is a messenger [apostle] greater than the one who sent him."

4. Apostle = the 12 Apostles in the Book of Acts

Acts 1:2; 1:26; 2:37, 42, 43; 4:33, 35, 37; 5:12, 29, 40; 6:6; 8:1, 14, 18; 9:27; 11:1; 15:2, 4, 6, 22, 23; 16:4. Among them the following are noteworthy:
Acts 2:43; 5:12: "... miraculous signs were done by the apostles" (compare 2 Corinthians 12:12 in point 7).
Acts 2:42: They devoted themselves to the apostles' teaching ..."
Acts 11:1: "The apostles and the brothers ..."
Acts 15:2, 4, 6, 22, 23; 16:4: "... the apostles and elders ..."

---

[75] Also see Peter van Deun, "The Notion *apostolikos*: A Terminological Survey," in *The Apostolic Age in Patristic Thought*, ed. A. Hilhorst (Leiden: Brill, 2004), 41–50.

5. Apostle = Peter in the first verse of Peter's epistles

1 Peter 1:1; 2 Peter 1:1

6. Apostle = Paul in the first verse of Paul's epistles

Romans 1:1; 1 Corinthians 1:1; 2 Corinthians 1:1; Galatians 1:1; Ephesians 1:1; Colossians 1:1; 1 Timothy 1:1; 2 Timothy 1:1; Titus 1:1 (Texts can be found in part under point 8).

7. Apostle = the 12 Apostles and Paul in the Epistles of Paul

1 Corinthians 4:9: "For it seems to me that God has put us apostles on display at the end of the procession, like men condemned to die in the arena. We have been made a spectacle to the whole universe, to angels as well as to men."
1 Corinthians 9:5: "Don't we have the right to take a believing wife along with us, as do the other apostles and the Lord's brothers and Cephas?"
1 Corinthians 15:9: "For I am the least of the apostles and do not even deserve to be called an apostle, because I persecuted the church of God."
2 Corinthians 11:5: "But I do not think I am in the least inferior to those 'super-apostles.'"
2 Corinthians 12:12: "The things that mark an apostle – signs, wonders and miracles – were done among you with great perseverance."
Galatians 1:17: "... nor did I go up to Jerusalem to see those who were apostles before I was ..."
Galatians 1:19: "I saw none of the other apostles – only James ..."

8. Apostle = Paul in Paul's Epistles

Romans 1:1: "Paul, a servant of Christ Jesus, called to be an apostle and set apart for the gospel of God ..."
Romans 11:13: "Inasmuch as I am the apostle to the Gentiles, I make much of my ministry."
1 Corinthians 1:1: "Paul, called to be an apostle of Christ Jesus by the will of God ..."
1 Corinthians 9:1: "Am I not free? Am I not an apostle? Have I not seen Jesus our Lord? Are you not the result of my work in the Lord?"

2 Biblical-Systematic Section

> 1 Corinthians 9:2: "Even though I may not be an apostle to others, surely I am to you!" (see point 9 for verse 2b)
>
> 2 Corinthians 1:1 = Ephesians 1:1 = Colossians 1:1: "Paul, an apostle of Christ Jesus by the will of God ..."
>
> 2 Corinthians 12:12: "The things that mark an apostle – signs, wonders and miracles – were done among you with great perseverance."
>
> Galatians 1:1: "Paul, an apostle – sent not from men nor by man, but by Jesus Christ and God the Father ..."
>
> Galatians 2:8: "For God, who was at work in the ministry of Peter as an apostle to the Jews, was also at work in my ministry as an apostle to the Gentiles."
>
> 1 Timothy 1:1: "Paul, an apostle of Christ Jesus by the command of God our Savior and of Christ Jesus our hope ..."
>
> 1Timothy 2:7: "And for this purpose I was appointed a herald and an apostle – I am telling the truth, I am not lying – and a teacher of the true faith to the Gentiles."
>
> 2 Timothy 1:1: "Paul, an apostle of Christ Jesus by the will of God, according to the promise of life that is in Christ Jesus ..."
>
> 2 Timothy 1:11: "And of this gospel I was appointed a herald and an apostle and a teacher."

9. "Apostolic Ministry" (here we find 'apostole' instead of 'apostolos')

> Acts 1:25: "... show us which of these two you have chosen to take over this apostolic ministry, which Judas left to go where he belongs" (by the election of Matthias, see verses 24, 26).
>
> Galatians 2:8: see point 8.
>
> Romans 1:5: "Through him and for his name's sake, we received grace and apostleship to call people from among all the Gentiles to the obedience that comes from faith."
>
> 1 Corinthians 9:2: "Are you not the result of my work in the Lord?" (verse 2a, see point 8).

10. Words of the Apostles

2 Peter 3:2: "I want you to recall the words spoken in the past by the holy prophets and the command given by our Lord and Savior through your apostles."

Jude 17: "But, dear friends, remember what the apostles of our Lord Jesus Christ foretold."

11. Apostle = the 12 Apostles in John's Revelation

Revelation 18:20: "Rejoice over her, O heaven! Rejoice, saints and apostles and prophets!"

Revelation 21:14: "The wall of the city had twelve foundations, and on them were the names of the twelve apostles of the Lamb."

12. "Apostles and Prophets"

1 Corinthians 12:28: "And in the church God has appointed first of all apostles, second prophets, third teachers, then ..."

1 Corinthians 12:29: "Are all apostles? Are all prophets? Are all teachers?"

Ephesians 2:20: "Consequently, you are ... built on the foundation of the apostles and prophets, with Christ Jesus himself as the chief cornerstone."

Ephesians 3:5: "[the mystery] which ... has now been revealed by the Spirit to God's holy apostles and prophets."

Ephesians 4:11: "It was he who gave some to be apostles, some to be prophets, some to be evangelists, and some to be pastors and teachers ..."

2 Peter 3: "I want you to recall the words spoken in the past by the holy prophets and the command given by our Lord and Savior through your apostles."

Revelation 18:20: "Rejoice over her, O heaven! Rejoice, saints and apostles and prophets! God has judged her for the way she treated you."

13. False Apostles

2 Corinthians 11:13: "For such men are false apostles, deceitful workmen, masquerading as apostles of Christ."

> Revelation 2:2: "I know ... that you have tested those who claim to be apostles but are not, and have found them false."[76]

14. Apostles = other apostles than the 12 Disciples and Paul

14.1. Leading Representatives of the Church in Jerusalem

Matthias, Acts 1:25: "Then they prayed, 'Lord, you know everyone's heart. Show us which of these two you have chosen to take over this apostolic ministry, which Judas left to go where he belongs" (Matthias was selected.).

James and Judas, 1 Corinthians 9:5: "Don't we have the right to take a believing wife along with us, as do the other apostles and the Lord's brothers and Cephas?" (James and Judas are placed on a par with the Apostles.).

James, Galatians 1:19: "I saw none of the other apostles – only James, the Lord's brother" (James is an apostle.).

1 Corinthians 15:5-7: Jesus appeared to James and to the Twelve; he appeared to more than 500 of the brothers and sisters; and "Then he appeared to James, then to all the apostles." (It is unclear whether James, the brother of Jesus, is seen here as an apostle or is only on a par with them.)

14.2. Co-workers of the Apostle Paul

Barnabas, Acts 14:4: "Some sided with the Jews, others with the apostles" (Barnabas is an apostle.).

Barnabas, Acts 14:14: "But when the apostles Barnabas and Paul heard of this ..." (Barnabas is an apostle.).

Andronicus and Junias, Romans 16:7: "Greet Andronicus and Junias. ... They are outstanding among the apostles ..."[77]

---

[76] Adolf Harnack, *Die Mission und Ausbreitung des Christentums in den ersten drei Jahrhunderten.* (Wiesbaden: VMA-Verlag, n.d., rpt. 1924), 335, correctly points out that "the polemic against pseudo-apostles and super-apostles demonstrates that the term 'apostle' is not a numerically defined term."

[77] Ibid, 335, and C. E. B. Cranfield, *A Critical and Exegetical Commentary on the Epistle to the Romans*, vol. 2 (Edinburgh: T. & T. Clark, 1989) 789-90, reject the alternative translation "outstanding among the apostles," whereby those named were themselves not apostles.

> Epaphroditus as a messenger of the church, Philippians 2:25: "... Epaphroditus, my brother, fellow worker and fellow soldier, who is also your messenger [apostle], whom you sent to take care of my needs."
>
> General messengers of the churches, 2 Corinthians 8:23: "... as for our brothers, they are representatives of the churches and an honor to Christ" (messengers of the churches in missions work are apostles).

Comments on the list: The closest disciples are labeled apostles (see points 2 and 3). In addition, Matthias is later a substitute for Judas (14), and then there is Paul (see 6 to 9). All these apostles saw Jesus (Paul via a vision), were commissioned by him, demonstrated their apostolic office by special signs and wonders (see 9 in particular), and played a part in the revelation and recording of the New Testament message (see 10 to 12).

Occasionally, other co-founders or leaders in the New Testament church are called apostles or are placed on a par with the apostles, including the brothers of Jesus, James and Judas (see 14), and possibly also Barnabas. In the case of Barnabas, this could be a matter of the general term apostle, which above all becomes clear in 2 Corinthians 8:23. There Paul speaks generally about "representatives of the churches" (see 14), possibly also Barnabas. Here the apostles are workers sent out generally for Paul's missionary work (see Philippians 2:25) with a leadership task that mostly encompasses several churches. They are not "apostles of Jesus Christ," as the apostles are sometimes designated in a narrower sense. Rather, they are "apostles of the churches." They best correspond to our present-day missionaries, whereby *missionary* is merely derived from the Latin translation of the Greek word *apóstolos* (messenger).

As important as this general task of apostles sent by the church is, one must bear in mind that wherever there is a mention of the words and commands of the apostles (see 10), the establishment of the New Testament church (see 11 and 12), or the revelation of the Word of God, the foundational apostles are meant.

For that reason, it is apparent that there could have been foundational apostles only in the generations during and after Jesus' time on earth. In contrast, there were still apostles in the sense of 2 Corinthians 8:23 in the second century A.D.,[78] and there are still apostles in that sense today.[79]

---

[78] Documented in Harnack, *Die Mission und Ausbreitung des Christentums*, 361.

[79] Also in the Middle Ages, the word *apostle* designated Jesus' 12 Apostles as well as all missionaries, according to Einar Molland, "Besaß die Alte Kirche ein Missionsprogramm?" (Did the Ancient Church Possess a Missions Program?) in *Die*

When Paul writes in Romans 15:19 that "from Jerusalem all the way around to Illyricum, I have fully proclaimed the gospel of Christ," he does not mean that he preached the gospel to every individual. Rather, it means that he had founded churches in all the strategically important locations. The same applies to the statement that "there is no more place for me to work in these regions" (verse 23). For that reason, Paul did not look for regions where Christ was known (verse 20) and where the gospel was already being preached. Rather, he looked for locations where no one had preached the gospel and no indigenous church existed. If mission work had followed Paul's model, the spiritual map would look much differently today.

In my opinion, based on these texts, we should clearly differentiate between two types of missionaries and not simply refer to all Christians who work overseas as being in the same category.

On one hand, in the precise or more narrow sense, there are missionaries such as those just described, those "not ... building on someone else's foundation." That means they preach the gospel where the gospel has never been preached or, more specifically, where there are no indigenous churches calling upon God's name (Romans 15:21).

On the other hand, there are Christians who contribute their profession, their gifts, and their involvement to churches and other works that are outside of their own cultural spheres. Although I do not wish to discount the sacrifices they make, they serve with a gift that they could and should also employ in their native surroundings, and they should find and become subject to a local church if at all possible. Unfortunately, this is too often not done.

The reason why this differentiation between missionaries in the precise sense and Christians who are active overseas in starting churches or in evangelism is so significant appears when one attempts to assign a percentage of all evangelical missionaries worldwide to each category. Of course, statistics are always to be handled with care; in this case, the results depend on how one defines "unreached peoples" and on how broadly one makes the category of evangelical missionaries. In any case, however, the trend is always pretty much the same: the percentage of missionaries seeking to bring the gospel to unreached peoples is very small.

Alte Kirche: Kirchengeschichte als Missionsgeschichte, vol. 1, ed. Heinzgünther Frohnes and Uwe W. Knorr (Munich: Chr. Kaiser, 1974), 57.

3 Confessional Section

The Filioque: Son and Spirit

At this point, a difference between the teaching of the Eastern Church and that of Western Christianity will be addressed that relates directly to the question of missio Dei.

Up to the present day, there have been two points upon which the Orthodox Church and the Catholic Church have not been able to agree, namely the meaning of the primacy of the pope (authoritatively or representatively) and the auxiliary *filioque* in the sole ecumenical confession of faith, the Niceno-Constantinopolitan Creed. In the latter instance, the question is whether the Holy Spirit proceeds only from the Father or from the Father and the Son. Only the latter question has to do with the other Western churches, including most Evangelical and Protestant churches.

In connection with his statement that "the Father sends the Son, and the Father and Son send the Holy Spirit for the salvation of humanity,"[80] Georg Vicedom views the Catholic and Protestant (and thus Western) position as self-evident and universally valid. The offshoot of this observation is that one could conclude from the salvific sending of the Spirit that the Holy Spirit proceeds in his eternal origin from the Father *and* the Son, as is expressed in the famous *filioque* (Latin for "and from the Son")[81] – an expression that played an important role in the split between Orthodox churches of the East and churches in the West.[82] The theology of the

---

[80] Vicedom, "Missio Dei," 352.
[81] In defense of the view of Western churches, see Barth, *Kirchliche Dogmatik*, vol. 1, 496–511; Alister E. McGrath, *Der Weg der christlichen Theologie* (Munich: C. H. Beck, 1997), 321–25 (Anglican); Francis Turretin, *Institutes of Elenctic Theology*, vol. 1 (Philipsburg, NJ: Presbyterian & Reformed, 1992), 308–19 (Chapter 3, Question 31) (Reformed); Johann Auer and Joseph Ratzinger, *Kleine katholische Dogmatik*, vol. 2: *Gott, der Eine und Dreieine* (Regensburg: Friedrich Pustet, 1978), 295–304 (Catholic); Colin Wright, "In Defense of Augustine: The *Filioque* Debate," *Christianity and Society* 8, no. 4 (1994): 20–23; sharper and more critically, Stephen J. Hayhow, "In Defense of the *Filioque*," *Christianity and Society* 8, no. 4 (1994): 23–25. (That the Eastern Church's lack of *filioque* is the reason for the Eastern Church's weakly developed soteriology and the reason why it did not experience a reformation are unfortunately only asserted but not documented.)
[82] The best brief historical presentation on the Confession and the addition of *filioque* is found in Reinhart Staats, *Das Glaubensbekenntnis von Nizäa-Konstantinopel*:

Eastern Church denies ancient Near Eastern[83] as well as Orthodox theology that claims that the Holy Spirit proceeds from the Son. Instead, it believes that the Spirit proceeds only from the Father. The Orthodox view of missio Dei is for that reason somewhat different.

The original Niceno-Constantinopolitan Creed, composed in Greek in 381 A.D., does not contain the filioque. The thought appeared for the first time in the first two great Western church theologians who wrote in Latin, Tertullian (died around 230 A.D.) and St. Augustine (died 430 A.D.; above all in *De Trinitate* II: 1, 3; II: 5, 7; IV: 20, 29; IV: 21,32). The former was active well before the Council of 381 A.D. and the latter after the Council.[84] The Council of Toledo in 589 A.D. discovered the importance of the Holy Spirit and added the filioque in the exegesis – but not in the text – of the confession.[85] The official dispute between the Western Church and the Eastern Church began at the Council of Nicea in 787 A.D., whereby the compromise proposed by the Patriarch Tarasios of Constantinople, the "Spirit from the Father through the Son," was adopted.[86] That formulation has been repeatedly suggested throughout all of theological history.[87]

Historische und theologische Grundlagen (Darmstadt: Wissenschaftliche Buchgesellschaft, 1996), 193–202. The most historical presentations on the *filioque* discussion are Bernd Oberdorfer, *Filioque: Geschichte und Theologie eines ökumenischen Problems* (Göttingen: Vandenhoeck & Ruprecht, 2001) and Peter Gemeinhardt *Die Filioque-Kontroverse zwischen Ost- und Westkirche im Frühmittelalter: Arbeiten zur Kirchengeschichte* 82 (Berlin: de Gruyter, 2002). The more recent era is the focus of Maria-Helene Gamillscheg, *Die Kontroverse um das Filioque: Möglichkeiten einer Problemlösung auf Grund der Forschungen und Gespräche der letzten hundert Jahre. Das östliche Christentum* NF 45 (Würzburg: Augustinus-Verlag, 1996). See also Alfred Stirnemann and Gerhard Wilflinger (eds.), *Vom Heiligen Geist: Der gemeinsame trinitarische Glaube und das Problem des Filioque* (Innsbruck and Vienna: Tyrolia, 1998); Dietrich Ritschl, "Geschichte der Kontroverse um das Filioque," *Concilium* 15 (1979): 499–509; and Jürgen Moltmann, *Trinität und Reich Gottes: Zur Gotteslehre* (Munich: Chr. Kaiser, 1986), 194–206.

[83] See representatively the Armenian-Orthodox view in Mesrob K. Kirkorian, "Das römische Dokument über den Ausgang des Heiligen Geistes aus orientalisch-orthodoxer Sicht," in *Die Armenische Kirche: Materialien zur armenischen Geschichte*, ed. Mesrob K. Kirkorian (Frankfurt: Peter Lang, 2007), 159–71, reprinted in Stirnemann and Wilflinger, *Vom Heiligen Geist*, 125–40; Sergio La Porta, "The 'Filioque' Controversy in Armenia," *Saint Nersess Theological Review* 8 (2003): 85–116.

[84] According to Staats, *Das Glaubensbekenntnis von Nizäa-Konstantinopel*, 196.

[85] Ibid, 194.

[86] Ibid, 196.

[87] See documentation in Oberdorfer, *Filioque*.

3 Confessional Section

"The Niceno-Constantinopolitan Creed (Latin: Symbolum Nicaeno-Constantinopolitanum) is the sole unifying confession of faith applicable to world-Christianity and mutually acknowledged by the Western and Eastern Churches. It is traceable back to the Second Ecumenical Council of Constantinople (381 A.D.) and expands the *Nicene Creed* arising from the First Ecumenical Council of Nicea (325 A.D.). In Orthodox churches, the Niceno-Constantinopolitan Creed is the central liturgical confession of faith. In the Catholic church it is prayed in mass as the Large Confession of Faith (*Credo*), and in the Anglican Church and a number of Evangelical churches it is used on high holidays in place of the *Apostolicum*."[88]

Until the time of Charlemagne, however, the filioque was not added to the official text of the confession of faith in the West. Rather, it only counted as its correct exegesis. Charlemagne first exacted adoption of the wording in the confession from the Pope, and Emperor Henry II, 200 years later, required adoption of the supplement into the liturgical mass.[89] The filioque was a topic of the Fourth Council of Constantinople from 879 to 880 A.D., which confirmed the confession of faith of 381 A.D. and declared a number of auxiliary wordings to be invalid. In 1014, Pope Benedict VIII added the filioque to the text of the confession with ecclesiastical authority. The filioque played a central role in the bilateral excommunication of the Pope and the Patriarch of Constantinople in 1054, the date of the official split between the Western and Eastern Churches. However, the Catholic Church first lifted the addition of the filioque to the level of dogma at the Fourth Lateran Council in 1215.

To the Orthodox churches, the filioque is a one-sided change to a ruling by a generally recognized ecumenical council and contradicts their view of the Trinity. The Orthodox view[90] denies that a person within the

---

[88] Schirrmacher, "Lexikon des Christentums," 204–5.
[89] Ibid, 197–201.
[90] For instance, the Greek Orthodox point of view is well described by Vladimir Lossky, "The Procession of the Holy Spirit in Orthodox Trinitarian Orthodoxy," in Lossky, *In the Image and Likeness of God* (Crestwood, NY: St. Vladimir's Seminary Press, 2001), 71–96; George Dion Dragas, "The Eighth Ecumenical Council: Constantinople IV (879/880) and the Condemnation of the Filioque Addition and Doctrine," *Greek Orthodox Theological Review* 44 (1999): 357–69, now at www.geocities.com/trvalentine/orthodox/dragas_eighth.html; and "Das römische Dokument über den Ausgang des Heiligen Geistes aus orthodoxer Sicht," in *Vom Heiligen Geist: Der gemeinsame trinitarische Glaube und das Problem des Filioque*, ed. Alfred Stirnemann and Gerhard Wilflinger (Innsbruck: Tyrolia, 1998), 141–86. An example of a modern Eastern Church presentation is the clear subordination viewpoint of the Greek Orthodox Metropolitan of Pergamon, John D. Zizioulas, *Being as Communion: Studies in Personhood and the Church* (Crestwood, NY: St. Vla-

Trinity (Jesus) can in a complete sense proceed from a person within the Trinity (the Father) while simultaneously, in a complete sense, having another person within the Trinity proceed from himself. Orthodox theology thus differentiates between the Holy Spirit as being *sent* from the Father and the Son, which they accept, and the Holy Spirit as *proceeding* from the Father and from the Son, which they reject, by teaching that the Spirit like the Son proceeds only from the Father.

The Orthodox churches primarily assert three points against the filioque:

1) Through the inclusion of "and the Son," multiple origins are claimed within God. The Father, however, is the sole source within the Trinity. The Son and the Holy Spirit should be considered as the right and left arms of the Father. The Son is "begotten" (*generatio*), whereas the Spirit is "breathed out" (*spiratio*). For Orthodox theology, there cannot be two sources of the Godhead, but only one.
2) The inclusion of the filioque gives the impression that the Holy Spirit was first called into life through Jesus. Indeed, Jesus announces that the Holy Spirit will be sent to people (John 14:16–17). That does not mean, however, that the Holy Spirit did not exist beforehand (see, for example, Psalm 51:13).
3) The filioque leads to submission of the Spirit to the Father and the Son. In the Western tradition, the teaching on the Holy Spirit has been treated as marginal. This has so-called Christomonism as a consequence.

For Western churches, the biblical passages cited to defend their point of view are above all John 14:26 and 15:26, and Luke 24:49, whereby these texts only apply if one proceeds on the assumption that one may infer the intrinsic, eternal (immanent) Trinity from this accomplishment (the sending of the Holy Spirit) in salvation history (the economic Trinity) and conclude from the sending of the Spirit through the Son to what is likewise the "proceeding" of the Spirit in eternity from the Son. Over the past centuries and up to the present day, however, this claim, that we can draw conclusions regarding the immanent Trinity from we know regard-

---

dimir's Seminary Press, 1993), 41. The most comprehensive compilation of the points of view of Orthodox (also Russian Orthodox and ancient Near Eastern) theologians on the topic in German is found in Oberdorfer, *Filioque*, 419–506.

3 Confessional Section 69

ing the economic Trinity, has been and is still disputed in Western theology by many a theologian.[91]

The 1995 statement by the Vatican, "The Greek and Latin Traditions regarding the Procession of the Holy Spirit: Pontifical Council for Promoting Christian Unity," was a significant step.[92] This clarification proceeds upon the assumption that the Greek Bible text *para tou patros ekporeuetai* (John 15:26) was rendered completely differently in the Latin Vulgate with the words *qui a Patre procedit*, and that for that reason the Greek text of the Niceno-Constantinopolitan Creed, *ek tou Patros ekporeuomenon*, became *ex Patre procedit* in Latin. In the process it should be noted that the Greek word *ekporeuetai* specifically means origin whereas the Latin word *procedere* more generally means proceedings of all types.[93] The two understandings vary, but they are not contradictory.[94]

According to the Catholic "clarification," the controversy surrounding the filioque no longer belongs to the dogmatic core of Catholic teaching and has to do with complementary and not mutually exclusive points of view in the case of the Western and Eastern churches. The Vatican points out that the Orthodox have often been quite content to formulate it as follows: "who has his origin from the Father through the Son" (*dia*).[95] The filioque may not be taught in such a manner that the monarchy of

---

[91] Oberdorfer, *Filioque*, 571–72 represents an unusual view, namely that the economic Trinity always implies the essential and that, however, in the case of salvific "sending" it is a matter of something other than eternal, essential "proceeding." But a question remains: If that is so, which eternal characteristic is implied by the sending of the Spirit?

[92] "Die griechische und die lateinische Überlieferung über den Ausgang des Heiligen Geistes: Eine Klarstellung in Verantwortung des Päpstlichen Rates zur Förderung der Einheit der Christen," *Una Sancta* 50, no. 4 (1995): 316–24, reprinted in Stirnemann and Wilflinger (eds.), *Vom Heiligen Geist*, 23–34. See also David Coffey, "The Roman 'Clarification' of the Doctrine of the Filioque," *International Journal of Systematic Theology* 5 (2003): 3–21, and Waclaw Hryniewicz, "Versöhnung im Trinitarischen Glauben? Die römisch-katholische Klarstellung über den Ausgang des Heiligen Geistes," in *Vom Heiligen Geist: Der gemeinsame trinitarische Glaube und das Problem des Filioque*, ed. Alfred Stirnemann and Gerhard Wilflinger (Innsbruck: Tyrolia, 1998), 53–71.

[93] "Die griechische und die lateinische Überlieferung," 318–19.

[94] Oberdorfer, *Filioque*, 532–41 has correctly noted that at this point the Catholic Church simply assumes that the Latin Niceno-Constantinopolitan Creed is a different confession from the Greek one! He also points out that, as is generally known, the Catholic Church does not negate what has been proclaimed earlier; rather, it always achieves changes through interpretation and extension.

[95] "Die griechische und die lateinische Überlieferung," 317.

the Father is placed into question, which would then contradict what John 15:26 expressly teaches (Greek: *ek monou tou patros*).[96]

On the other hand, there has been vehement opposition to giving up the content of the filioque especially from the Lutheran side,[97] even if in the case of worship services together with Orthodox Churches the addition of the filioque has been dispensed with. Indeed, the Eighth Assembly of the Lutheran World Federation in Curitiba in 1990 recommended dispensing with the filioque in ecumenical worship services, along with allowing editions of the confession of faith without the filioque in the vernacular in countries with a strongly Orthodox segment of the population. However, with regard to substance, the Western church position remains clearly supported.[98] The Evangelical Lutheran Church of Germany (Vereinigte Evangelisch-Lutherisch Kirche Deutschlands, or VELKD) has even more clearly defended this position.[99]

For the Lutheran Bernd Oberdorfer, liturgically dispensing with the filioque, for example, is possible only if the Orthodox churches expressly do not hold the filioque to be heretical and if they acknowledge the Western Church and Protestant motive for the filioque, do not relativize the emphasis on the Christological determination of the Spirit, and do not relativize the cross of Jesus over against his resurrection.[100]

Jürgen Moltmann has essentially posed the question of why the Reformers and the early Reformed churches did not review the filioque and did not take up discussion with the Orthodox Church.[101] However, the Lutheran Ulrich Kühn has correctly emphasized that the filioque was always so important to the Reformation because the Reformers saw in it the guarantee that salvation effected by the Son was then conveyed

---

[96] Ibid, 318.
[97] For example, Oberdorfer, *Filioque*, 557–65; Reinhard Slenczka, "Das Filioque in der neueren ökumenischen Diskussion," in *Glaubensbekenntnis und Kirchengemeinschaft: Das Modell des Konzils von Konstantinopel (381)*, ed. Karl Lehmann et al. (Freiburg: Herder, 1982), 80–99; Ulrich Kühn, "Die Wiederentdeckung der Wirklichkeit des Geistes – Ein Votum aus lutherischer Sicht," in *Vom Heiligen Geist: Der gemeinsame trinitarische Glaube und das Problem des Filioque*, ed. Alfred Stirnemann and Gerhard Wilflinger (Innsbruck and Vienna: Tyrolia, 1998), 72–80.
[98] *Ökumenisch den Glauben bekennen: Das Nicaeno-Constantinopolitanum von 381 als verbindendes Glaubensbekenntnis - Stellungnahme der VELKD* 139/2007, November 2007, available at: http://www.velkd.de/publikationen/publikationen-gesamtkatalog.php?publikation=346&kategorie=22. See especially pages 30 and 31.
[99] Ibid; see primarily the criticism of a broader opening in the commentary of the Theological Committee of the VELKD, especially pages 44–52.
[100] Oberdorfer, *Filioque*, 560.
[101] Moltmann, *Trinität und Reich Gottes*, 195.

through the Spirit and that in addition to this salvation in Christ there could not be in any measure a parallel and independently running fellowship with the Father through the Spirit.[102]

Reformed theologians, most comprehensively Karl Barth, have likewise continued to defend the filioque, even if in recent times there has been some pleading in favor of dispensing with the additional wording in joint worship services with Orthodox churches.[103]

What is primarily central for Barth, as for most Western theologians after him, is identifying the economic (salvific-historical) Trinity with the immanent (essential) Trinity.[104] In addition, Barth emphasized in particular that the Spirit does not have a double origin in the Father and the Son but rather a sole joint origin in both. Because as a Spirit of love he embodies the essence of a loving fellowship, he can also only proceed from his own fellowship.[105]

From a Western church point of view, the *locus classicus* – for Martin Luther, for instance – is John 16:7–15.[106] In addition, Philipp Melanchthon felt that John 15:26 and 20:22 were clear on this point. According to Jesus' words (John 16:14), the Holy Spirit takes everything from Jesus and proclaims nothing other than Jesus himself. These texts, however, are also understood today by Western church theologians more in salvific terms, thus having to do with the historical sending and not the origin of the Spirit. (Moreover, two different Greek verbs, *erchomai* and *exporeuomai*,

---

[102] Kühn, "Die Wiederentdeckung der Wirklichkeit des Heiligen Geistes," 75.
[103] See the nuanced presentation by Robert Letham, *Through Western Eyes: Eastern Orthodoxy, A Reformed Perspective* (Fearn: GB, 2007), 224–42, and Robert Letham, *The Holy Trinity: In Scripture, History, Theology, and Worship* (Philipsburg, NJ: Presbyterian & Reformed, 2004), 201–20. See also Ulrich H. J. Körner, "'Der Herr ist der Geist' – das römische Dokument und sein Beitrag zum ökumenischen Gespräch aus reformierter Sicht," in *Vom Heiligen Geist: Der gemeinsame trinitarische Glaube und das Problem des Filioque*, ed. Alfred Stirnemann and Gerhard Wilflinger (Innsbruck and Vienna: Tyrolia, 1998), 81–96, especially 81–82 with reference to the Reformers. Körner writes, "Als Pneumatologen im engeren Sinne aber unter den Reformatoren vor allem U. Zwingli, M. Bucer und J. Calvin bezeichnet warden" (Above all, among the Reformers, however, U. Zwingli, M. Bucer, and J. Calvin would be considered pneumatologists in the narrow sense of the word) along with Karl Barth (pp. 85–87).
[104] In particular, Barth, *Kirchliche Dogmatik*, vol. 1, 503, and Körner, "Der Herr ist der Geist," 85–89.
[105] Barth, *Kirchliche Dogmatik*, vol. 1., 510. For a criticism of Barth's position and his dealings with the Orthodox position, see Oberdorfer, *Filioque*, 350–71.
[106] Also according to Staats, *Das Glaubensbekenntnis von Nizäa-Konstantinopel*, 195–96.

are used for Christ's going forth in John 8:42 and the Spirit's going forth in John 15:26.)[107]

Just how multifaceted the formulation of the relationship of the Spirit to the Father and to the Son with respect to sending and origin can be is shown in the following table.

The Sending of the Spirit with various References to the Father and the Son

John 14:26: "But the Counselor, the Holy Spirit, whom the Father will send in my name. ..." (The Father sends the Spirit, but in the name of the Son.)
John 15:26: "When the Counselor comes, whom I will send to you from the Father, the Spirit of truth who goes out from the Father, he will testify about me." (Jesus sends the Spirit, but does so from the Father.)
John 16:7: "It is for your good that I am going away. Unless I go away, the Counselor will not come to you; but if I go, I will send him to you." (Jesus sends the Spirit.)
John 16:15: "All that belongs to the Father is mine. That is why I said the Spirit will take from what is mine and make it known to you." (The Spirit takes everything from the Son because the Son takes everything from the Father.)
1 Corinthians 2:12: "We have not received the spirit of the world but the Spirit who is from God, that we may understand what God has freely given us." (The Spirit proceeds from God, which can collectively mean the Father or God.)

In the New Testament, the Spirit is called the "the Spirit of God" (Romans 8:9; 1 Corinthians 3:16; John 14:26; 1 Peter 4:14), "the Spirit of your Father" (Matthew 10:20), and "the Spirit of Christ" (2 Corinthians 3:17; 1 Corinthians 15:45; Romans 8:9; Galatians 4:6; 1 Peter 1:11), whereas the terms are used in parallel in Romans 8:9. Paul's distinctly Trinitarian manner of presenting the Spirit as an independent quantity in Romans 8:9–16, as the Spirit of Christ, the Spirit of God, the Spirit as Christ in us, and the "Spirit of sonship," which conveys our true relationship to the Father, merits careful attention:

> "You, however, are controlled not by the sinful nature but by the Spirit, if the Spirit of God lives in you. And if anyone does not have the Spirit of

---

[107] Also according to Auer and Ratzinger, *Kleine katholische Dogmatik*, vol. 2, 295.

Christ, he does not belong to Christ. But if Christ is in you, your body is dead because of sin, yet your spirit is alive because of righteousness. And if the Spirit of him who raised Jesus from the dead is living in you, he who raised Christ from the dead will also give life to your mortal bodies through his Spirit, who lives in you … because those who are led by the Spirit of God are sons of God. For you did not receive a spirit that makes you a slave again to fear, but you received the Spirit of sonship. And by him we cry, 'Abba, Father.' The Spirit himself testifies with our spirit that we are God's children" (Romans 8:9–11, 14–16).

The following consideration, primarily from Karl Barth and Jürgen Moltmann, also accommodates the Western church view: The proceeding of the Spirit from the Father presupposes that the Father already is Father, and thus that the Son's proceeding from the Father is taken for granted.[108]

Even if there is a certain exegetical basis for the Western church view,[109] it is so thin that the filioque should surely not belong to the central truths of the faith.

For that reason, the compromise of 787 A.D. that the "Spirit [proceeds] from the Father through the Son" might best summarize the biblical facts.[110] The Catholic Church and the Lutheran World Federation also see it that way today (as noted above), for which reason both recommend dispensing with the filioque in ecumenical settings involving Orthodox Christians. Even the Lambeth Conference of the Anglican Church decided in 1988 to strike the filioque from future amended editions of liturgy without giving up the filioque with regard to content. In addition, churches of the Union of Utrecht (Old Catholic Churches and Christian Catholics) have completely deleted the filioque from the confession and liturgy as well as with regard to content.[111]

---

[108] See Moltmann, *Trinität und Reich Gottes*, 200–201.
[109] Dennis Ngien, *Apologetic for Filioque in Medieval Theology* (Carlisle: Paternoster, 2005), does a good job of presenting the exegetical reasons for the filioque brought forth particularly by Anselm of Canterbury, Richard of St. Victor, St. Thomas Aquinas, and St. Bonaventure. On the exegesis of relevant New Testament texts, see Oberdorfer, *Filioque*, 37–57.
[110] Moltmann, *Trinität und Reich Gottes*, 199 (see the entire discussion on pp. 194–206). On p. 203 he summarizes his suggestion: "The Holy Spirit, which proceeds from the Father of the Son and receives his character from the Father and the Son." According to p. 195, the filioque apparently "prevents the development of a Trinitarian pneumatology" (die Entwicklung einer trinitarischen Pneumatologie behindert).The justification of this is not completely clear to me.
[111] See Oberdorfer, *Filioque*, 296–349.

In the enormously extensive modern ecumenical filioque discussion,[112] it has hardly ever been made a topic of discussion that taken on the whole, modern Orthodox theology has not shown movement of any kind. The Western churches are looking for a solution, not the Eastern churches.[113] The western churches have dropped the heresy charge, but the Eastern churches have not. Even the fact that the Old Catholic Church dogmatically made the Orthodox position its own and completely struck the filioque dogmatically and with regard to content has, to my knowledge, never truly been acknowledged. Also, in the Old Catholic and Orthodox conversations there have never been real attempts at rapprochement[114] from the Orthodox side.

In conclusion, let us offer warning against saying more on the topic than revelation enables us to say by quoting the church father Cyril of Jerusalem (315–386 A.D.): "The Holy Spirit himself has dictated the Scriptures. He has also said everything about himself which he wanted to say or which we might be able to understand. Let us thus say what he said, and let us not dare to advance what he has not said."[115]

Missio Dei and Orthodox Theology

A central element of the biblical view of mission is that the individual doing the sending becomes the one sent, and that the one sent himself becomes the sending one. The only matter that remains unclear is whether one can carry this over to the eternal essence of the Trinity, thus as an eternal going out from the Father.

For that reason, the Orthodox and ancient Near Eastern view of the filioque does not mean that Orthodox theology is not acquainted with the Trinitarian justification of mission as missio Dei. For instance, the Ortho-

---

[112] On ecumenical dialogue in the 20th century, see Gamillscheg, *Die Kontroverse um das Filioque*; Oberdorfer, *Filioque*; Stirnemann and Wilflinger, *Vom Heiligen Geist*. On the most recent ecumenical discussions, see Lothar Lies, "Derzeitige ökumenische Bemühungen um das 'Filioque,'" *Zeitschrift für katholische Theologie* 122 (2000): 317–53; Peter Gemeinhardt, "Die Filioque-Kontroverse: historische Spurensuche und ökumenische Perspektiven," *Materialdienst des Konfessionskundlichen Instituts Bensheim* 54 (2003): 43–49; Bernd Oberdorfer, "Brauchen wir das Filioque? Aspekte des Filioque-Problems in der heutigen Diskussion," *Kerygma und Dogma* 49 (2003): 278–92; Hans Georg Thümmel, "Filioque," *Theologische Rundschau* 72 (2007112–20.

[113] See comments by the most important advocates in Oberdorfer, *Filioque*, 419–506.

[114] Oberdorfer, *Filioque*, 296–349.

[115] Quoted in Gamillscheg, *Die Kontroverse um das Filioque*, 13.

dox theologian Ion Bria writes the following in his chapter entitled "Die Bedeutung der trinitarischen Theologie" ("The Significance of Trinitarian Theology") in his book *Orthodoxe Perspectiven zur Mission* (*Orthodox Perspectives on Missions*):

> "The mission of the church is founded upon the mission of Christ. In the first instance, an appropriate understanding of this mission requires application of Trinitarian theology. Christ's sending of the apostles is rooted in the fact that Christ himself is sent in the Holy Spirit by the Father (John 20:21-23). The importance of this Biblical affirmation for the concept of mission is generally recognized, but the Trinitarian theology included in it merits more attention that it normally receives. Trinitarian theology points to the fact that God in himself illustrates a life of community and that God's involvement in history aims at pulling in humanity and the creation in general into this fellowship with God's very own life. The consequences of this affirmation are extremely important for the understanding of missions: Missions do not in the first instance target the propagation and passing on of intellectual convictions, teachings, ethical commands, etc. Rather, it is a matter of passing on the life of community which exists in God. The 'sending' associated with missions is essentially the sending of the Spirit (John 14:26), which really demonstrates the life of God as community" (1 Corinthians 13:13).[116]

Missio Dei and Catholic Theology

Anna Marie Aagaard has demonstrated that missio Dei was initially completely seized upon as a purely Protestant, missiological term in the Second Vatican Council's missions[117] decree entitled *Ad Gentes*.[118] There one reads the following after the introduction at the beginning of the main section: "The pilgrim Church is missionary by her very nature, since it is

---

[116] Ion Bria (ed.), *Go Forth in Peace: Orthodox Perspectives on Mission* (Geneva: World Council of Churches, 1986), 3; also Paulos Mar Gregorios, *The Meaning and Nature of Diakonia* (Geneva: World Council of Churches, 1988).

[117] Anna Marie Aagaard, "Missio Dei in katholischer Sicht: Missionstheologische Tendenzen," *Evangelische Theologie* 34 (1974): 421 poses a question that is answered positively without qualification: "The first thing which we can say about the term mission Dei is that it is Protestant new coinage in the theology of missions ... the question is now to be asked whether one can legitimately transfer such a Protestant term to the Catholic theology of missions and whether one can speak of mission Dei from a Catholic point of view."

[118] Karl Rahner and Herbert Vorgrimler, *Kleines Konzilskompendium: Sämtliche Texte des Zweiten Vatikanums* (Freiburg: Herder, 1985), 607-53.

from the mission of the Son and the mission of the Holy Spirit that she draws her origin, in accordance with the decree of God the Father. This decree, however, flows from the 'fount-like love' or charity of God the Father."[119]

Aagaard comments on the entire first chapter of *Ad Gentes*:

> "'The pilgrim Church is missionary by her very nature' – natura sua missionaria est. It is part of the essence of the church that it exists 'as an envoy on its way.' Because the church has been founded through the sending of the Son and the Spirit into the world, everything that the church is and does has mission as its signature. Since the Son and the Spirit have been sent into the world, the church originated in the world, and it exists only as the church on the basis of the presence of the sent Son and the sent Spirit. With these statements a sending-specific ecclesiology is expressed. Sending is what determines the church and not the other way around. A mission is not simply something which the church has. Because the church is constituted through the presence of God sent into the world, the church is a mission."[120]

A close connection is pointed to between the understanding of mission and teaching on the Trinity:

> "Yet just as ecclesiology is determined by missiology, so is missiology determined by the doctrine of the Trinity. The church can never be lord over its own mission and place the justification of mission into question. In so doing it would place its own existence into question. It only has its existence in God who was sent into the world as the Son and the Spirit. In the end it is God who sends. *Ad Gentes* says that it is namely out of his love that God wished to send the Son and the Spirit into the world. With that, God wanted to send his love into the world in order to lead the entire creation back to the love from which everything proceeds. The mission of the church is thus designated as a participant in the sending of God's love into the world in Word and Spirit. The church not only operates in mission because the Resurrected One commanded this. The church is so constituted through God's presence in sending. For that reason, it is in mission and cannot be anything else."[121]

---

[119] Ibid, 608 (= p. 2 of the article), chap. 1, par. 1; on the sending of the Spirit, p. 610 (= p. 4), chap. 1, par. 4.
[120] Aagaard, "Missio Dei in katholischer Sicht," 423.
[121] Ibid, 423.

However, it is not only the church that can be nothing other than missional (missionary). Rather, God himself is in his essence missional, and the doctrine of the Trinity, as the heart of Christian dogmatics, cannot be conveyed without mission.

> "Missiological statements do not only bind the church and mission together with the sending of the Word and the Spirit. Rather, they are bound together with the essence of the Triune God himself. The sending of divine persons into the world is indissolubly bound up with the proceeding of the Son and the Holy Spirit out of the inner life of the Trinity. In the Trinity the Son is begotten of the Father, and the Holy Spirit proceeds from the Father and the Son. These movements or 'proceedings' within the Trinity comprise the deepest reason for the sending or 'missions' of the Son and of the Holy Spirit. The introductory section of *Ad Gentes* thus states that the mission of the church has its basis in the sending of the Word and the Spirit. The sending of the Word and the Spirit, however, have their basis in the inner life of the Trinity. It is impossible to go further back than this. If one designates mission to be established in the life form of the Trinity itself, one is saying that mission necessarily is the life form of the church. The Council has thus determined that the church necessarily has to conduct missions, even if this mission can be problematic in the shape it takes."[122]

Aagaard has correctly pointed out that a mission justification takes priority. This has always been obvious dogmatically, but astonishingly it has only now become an acute issue.

> "With these words, *Ad Gentes* reflects the situation in which the decree occurred. This situation is marked by the fact that the earlier justification of the activity of missions no longer suffices. At the beginning of the century, one said that the church conducted mission in order to save souls. 'Conversio gentium' was the motivation of missions. In the 1940s and 1950s one used to speak about 'planting the church.' 'Plantatio ecclesiae' was the motivation for missions. However, these justifications did not suffice when one began to ask questions about the salvific actions of God outside the church. If God has other ways to people than the way of the church, it is absurd to maintain that missions work is absolutely necessary in order to save people. And if God has other ways to people than the way of the church, 'plantatio ecclesiae' cannot be a sufficient reason for the church's always having to conduct missions everywhere. The Council fathers were in a situation where Catholic mission theology – with researchers such as Hans Küng, among others – began to speak to people of many ways of sal-

---

[122] Ibid, 423–24.

vation. Thus, a new justification for missions had to be found if one wanted to hold firmly to an indispensable missional necessity. This justification was found in the theologically Trinitarian answer to the question: What is mission?"[123]

In short, "The Council succeeded by producing a connection between church and mission, between ecclesiology and mission theology. And this was achieved by making Trinitarian theology the overriding determinant for statements about the church as well as about mission."[124]

Aagaard has certainly pointed to the great problems and dangers of *Ad Gentes* as anchored in the Catholic understanding of the church.[125] In the Catholic understanding, the mission of the Spirit only occurs through the church – specifically, the structured Roman Catholic Church – such that the question arises as to whether the Holy Spirit is solely bound to this one organized church.

---

[123] Ibid, 424.
[124] Ibid, 423; see pp. 422–24 for further details.
[125] Ibid, 424–26.

Appendix: On the Term "Missional"

Much of what I have defended in this book has increasingly been labeled "missional" over the past ten years or so in place of the older term "missionary." That is not completely coincidental, since in the case of almost all advocates of the expression "missional church" the names Lesslie Newbigin and David Bosch are mentioned as the sources of inspiration and the representatives of the term's use. Both individuals were closely allied with the term *missio Dei*. Stefan Schweyer traces the concept of *missional* back to the missio Dei concept.[126]

The oldest documented evidence of the term's use has been dated to 1883 or perhaps 1814.[127] However, the term has been used by an enormous spectrum of proponents. Additionally, there have been many in the past who did not conceive of the term *missionary* as referring to the organized activities of missionary societies and churches. Rather, they conceived of it in a more comprehensive manner, as the missionary nature of the church per se. This is the idea that the church completely engages with the society and transforms it, thus precisely reflecting that which the term *missional* is supposed to underscore.

It is naturally poor form to transport a differentiation between *missionary* and *missional* back a number of centuries to a time when the latter term was not even available, or to discredit every individual who still utilizes the former term. And in practice it was even often worse: As a rule, whoever spoke about a missionary church meant the nature of the church and not canvassing for a large organization.

Reggie McNeal, for instance, announced in his book *Missional Renaissance* that a new golden age has dawned with the emergence of the missional church, the largest setting out since the Reformation. He wrote,

---

[126] Stefan Schweyer, "Kirche als Mission: Einsichten und Ausblicke zum Konzept der 'missional church,'" *Theologische Beilage zur STH-Postille*, February and March 2009; the same statement appeared at http://en.wikipedia.org/wiki/Missional as of July 7, 2010. Francis M. DuBose, *God Who Sends: A Fresh Quest for Biblical Mission* (Nashville, TN: Broadman, 1983), a classic on the justification of Trinitarian sending, refers on page 103 to "the missional call common to all Christians" and on page 110 to "the Missional Meaning of Worship."

[127] C. E. Bourne, *The Heroes of African Discovery and Adventure*, vol. 2: *From the Death of Livingstone to the Year 1882* (London: Swan Sonnenschein, 1886); for earlier sources, see the discussion at http://tallskinnykiwi.typepad.com/tallskinnykiwi/2008/01/missional-first.html.

"The rise of the missional church is the single biggest step development in Christianity since the Reformation."[128] In typically American fashion, this is expressed in superlatives ("The shifts are tectonic.").[129] I would, however, recommend awaiting the judgment of the next generation, when it can be seen whether something foundational has changed or if it is just a matter of a name change. One might enter this book into the records as typical American puffery: That which is decisive has now been discovered; everything up to now was only preliminary. That, however, changes nothing about the pretension it discloses.

But the check is still uncashed, so to speak. Typical evidence comes from McNeal's conclusion,[130] in which a group is mentioned as a prominent example of missional activity. It collected $10 million for the hungry and motivated 250,000 young people to enter into voluntary involvement. There is not a word about the hungry, not a word about which sustainable changes were brought about, and not a word about sinful structures that affect hunger. It was simply a program that boasts about money and numbers and conveys the sense that up to now, no one has been as good as we are. And that is supposed to be something unprecedented?

The central task, in the end, is described as asking *who* is the church instead of *what* is the church,[131] a typical Western, indeed English word play that cannot be biblically justified and does not correspond to the reality of how churches are growing in the global South, often in the face of bitter persecution. At this point, mission truly becomes identical with life. The statement is likewise nonsense historically, considering that, for instance, Calvin defined the church as the community of believers, thus describing it as not a *what* in terms of structures but a *who* in terms of people. In addition, the statement that "the missional understanding of Christianity is undoing Christianity as religion"[132] naturally sounds massive and perhaps could have its virtues if McNeal were to explain what he means by religion (e.g., spiritless Christianity, nominal Christianity, Karl Barth's Christianity brought about by people). However, as it stands, the missional life benefit remains equal to nothing.

---

[128] Reggie McNeal, *Missional Renaissance: Changing the Scorecard for the Church* (San Francisco, CA: Jossey-Bass, 2009), xiv.
[129] Ibid.
[130] Ibid, 177.
[131] Ibid, 148: "We need to change the conversation about the church from 'what is it?' to 'who is it?'"
[132] Ibid, xiv.

Appendix: On the Term "Missional"

Although his book is lacking as far as exegetical and theological foundations are concerned, McNeal does not want to see the dissolution of classical Christian theology: "The church has the apostolic function of exercising doctrinal oversight."[133] However, churches and their workers are no longer perceived as the community of Christ in their essence but, rather, are sought only for their utility in a new program.[134] In any case, McNeal incorrectly invokes David Bosch, Lesslie Newbigin, and the concept of missio Dei.[135]

Even if nowadays the "emerging church" movement uses the term 'missional' as a trademark and emphasizes the incarnational character of all mission and community, it should be noted that perhaps the earliest exponent of the term was Tim Keller,[136] a Reformed pastor of an innovative church in New York, Redeemer Presbyterian Church. The church is theologically very close to the approach recommended in this book.[137] The Lutheran World Federation likewise used the term "missional" in its 2004 declaration on mission[138] and declared: "Mission is the essence of the church, not only an activity of the church in addition to others. That is the basic message of the Lutheran World Federation's declaration entitled *Mission in Context*."[139]

Meanwhile, *missional* continues to mean a lot of things and even to have contrasting meanings. Some understand the word to denote a church that completely adapts incarnationally to its environment, whereas others understand just the opposite, a church offering an alternative community as an alternative draft of what society can be. Some understand *missional* to express a postmodern flexibility in questions of doctrine for the benefit of real relationships between people. Others presuppose an orthodox understanding of the mission of God in Christ lead-

---

[133] Ibid, 150.
[134] Ibid, 148–52.
[135] Ibid, 21–24.
[136] http://en.wikipedia.org/wiki/Missional, version dated July 7, 2010, ascribes the greatest influence in the spread of the term to be Tim Keller.
[137] See above all "The Missional Church," 2001, at http://www.redeemer2.com/resources/papers/missional.pdf. All publications and sermons by Tim Keller are listed at http://www.stevekmccoy.com/reformissionary/2005/07/tim_keller_arti.html.
[138] See Jürgen Quack, "Verwandeln, Versöhnen, Bevollmächtigen – Der Auftrag der Kirche in der Welt: Zur neuen Missionserklärung des Lutherischen Weltbundes," *Interkulturelle Theologie* 34 (2008): 313–14.
[139] Ibid, 305.

ing to everything being placed in the light of this mission and to everything being subordinated to it.

I would like to state it in the following way: I am very reluctant to think that a new term alone can do something new, and I seldom find anything in the literature advocating missional churches that has not already been said correctly and well for centuries. However, I am sympathetic to the content of what has been understood by the term, and the content is completely consonant with the reflections expressed in this book: mission is not an activity among others but constitutes the very essence of God and the church. It is what characterizes us individually and in community, and it extends from the incarnation of the Son of God through inner transformation of the individual to increasingly greater and more visible circles up to the transformation of the entire creation. I have documented this point extensively in a recent article.[140] For instance, when David Putman describes at length how one becomes a "missional follower of Jesus,"[141] I cannot relate to the undercurrent demonstrating a distinction between this and earlier notions. However, I can agree with what appears to be a somewhat reformulated version of what pietists wrote on the topic of "true sanctification" or what was understood in the 1960s by the term "true discipleship."

Francis M. DuBose wrote as early as 1993 in his book about the sending God, "Mission as sending has taught us that mission is not a type of Christian work. It is instead the work of God. For that reason, it is our work, the call upon our life."[142] Or, conversely: "There is no call to a Christian life separated from a call to mission."[143]

For instance, "12 Thesen zur missionalen Theologie"[144] (12 Theses on Missional Theology), published by IGW in Zürich, forgoes any polemics against others and simply describes how theology can only be understood as a setting out in a missionary sense. I can heartily agree with this. These authors argue almost exactly what I argued in my 30 theses entitled *Biblical*

---

[140] Thomas Schirrmacher, "Das biblische Mandat, die Welt zu retten – innerlich wie äußerlich – ganz privat und ganz global" (The Biblical Mandate to Save the World – Internally and Externally – Completely Personal and Completely Global) in *Transformierender Glaube*, ed. Andreas Kusch (Nürnberg: VTR, 2007), 19–34.

[141] David Putnam, *Breaking the Discipleship Code: Becoming a Missional Follower of Jesus* (Nashville, TN: B&H, 2009).

[142] DuBose, *God Who Sends*, 102.

[143] Ibid, 103.

[144] IGW International, "12 Thesen zur missionalen Theologie," http://blog.igw.edu/wp-content/uploads/2009/02/chre02-12-thesen-missionale-theologie-igw.pdf.

Reasons for Evangelical Missions, originally published in 1994.[145] That work was written at a time when the term *missional* was not yet in vogue.

Long before the term 'missional' became known and famous and missional principles were formulated, Emil Brunner in 1931 described the missional life of the church well in his *The Word and the World*.

"The Word of God which was given in Jesus Christ is a unique historical fact, and everything Christian is dependent on it; hence every one who receives this Word, and by it salvation, receives along with it the duty of passing this Word on; just as a man who might have discovered a remedy for cancer which saved himself, would be in duty bound to make this remedy accessible to all. *Mission work does not arise from any arrogance in the Christian Church; mission is its cause and its life. The Church exists by mission, just as a fire exists by burning. Where there is no mission, there is no Church; and where there is neither Church nor mission, there is no faith.* It is a secondary question whether by that we mean Foreign Missions, or simply the preaching of the Gospel in the home Church. Mission, Gospel preaching, is the spreading out of the fire which Christ has thrown upon the earth. He who does not propagate this fire shows that he is not burning. He who burns propagates the fire. This 'must' is both things - an urge and a command. An urge, because living faith feels God's purpose as its own. 'Woe is unto me, if I preach not the gospel,' says Paul. Necessity is laid upon him. But also he ought to preach; with the gift he receives the obligation. 'Go ye into all the world and preach the gospel'. Whether Christ's command was uttered just in these words, we do not know exactly. But there can be no doubt that He had sent out His disciples with the strict order to preach the gospel of the Kingdom to all the world. Even if Jesus had not done that, it would still be a divine command for every one who receives the message; for he knows that the divine remedy must be made accessible to all. The classical expression for this propagating activity is not doctrine but kerygma, i.e., the herald's call. The herald, the keryx, is a man who in the market-place of a city promulgates the latest decree of the king. He is the living publicity organ of the sovereign's will. The herald makes known what no one could know before: what the king has decreed. It is just this that the Apostles meant by kerygma. They brought not only good tidings, but new tidings as well."[146]

---

[145] Thomas Schirrmacher, "Biblische Grundlagen evangelikaler Missiologie: 30 Thesen," *Evangelikale Missiologie* 10, no. 4 (1994) 112–20. This document has been reprinted and translated; it is available in German, Dutch, and English as MBS Texts 55, 64, and 65, respectively, which can be downloaded at www.bucer.eu/mbstexte.html.

[146] Emil Brunner, *The Word and the World* (London: Student Christian Movement Press, 1931), 108, emphasis added.

About the Author

Prof. Dr. theol. Dr. phil. Thomas Schirrmacher, PhD, ThD, DD (born 1960), serves the World Evangelical Alliance [networking 600 million Protestants] as Associate Secretary General for Theological Concerns (responsible for Theology, Intrafaith and Interfaith Relations, Religious Freedom and Persecution) and as Chair of its Theological Commission.

As President of the International Council of the International Society for Human Rights (with sections in 55 countries), and as Director of the International Institute for Religious Freedom (Bonn, Cape Town, Colombo, São Paulo), Schirrmacher is one of the leading experts on human rights worldwide and regularly testifies in parliaments and courts worldwide, the OSCE and the UN in Geneva and New York.

Schirrmacher is visiting professor of the sociology of religion at the state University of the West in Timisoara (Romania) and Distinguished Professor of Global Ethics and International Development at William Carey University in Shillong (Meghalaya, India). He is president of 'Martin Bucer European Theological Seminary' (Bonn, Berlin, Prague, Istanbul, São Paulo), where he teaches ethics and comparative religions.

He studied theology from 1978 to 1982 at STH Basel (Switzerland) and since 1983 Cultural Anthropology and Comparative Religions at Bonn State University. He earned a Drs. theol. in Missiology and Ecumenics at Theological University (Kampen/Netherlands) in 1984, and a Dr. theol. in Missiology and Ecumenics at Johannes Calvin Foundation (Kampen/Netherlands) in 1985, a Ph.D. in Cultural Anthropology at Pacific Western University in Los Angeles (CA) in 1989, a Th.D. in Ethics at Whitefield Theological Seminary in Lakeland (FL) in 1996, and a Dr. phil. in Sociology of Religion at State University of Bonn in 2007. In 1997 he received an honorary doctorate (D.D.) from Cranmer Theological House, in 2006 one from Acts University in Bangalore.

His has authored and edited 102 books, which were translated into 17 languages, his newest dealing with 'Suppressed Women' (2015), 'Corruption' (2014), 'Human Rights' (2012), 'Human trafficking' (2011), 'Fundamentalism' (2010) and 'Racism' (2009).

He is listed in Marquis' Who's Who in the World, Dictionary of International Biography, International Who is Who of Professionals, 2000 Outstanding Intellectuals of the 21st Century, Kürschners Gelehrten-Kalender and other biographical year-books.

World Evangelical Alliance

World Evangelical Alliance is a global ministry working with local churches around the world to join in common concern to live and proclaim the Good News of Jesus in their communities. WEA is a network of churches in 129 nations that have each formed an evangelical alliance and over 100 international organizations joining together to give a worldwide identity, voice and platform to more than 600 million evangelical Christians. Seeking holiness, justice and renewal at every level of society – individual, family, community and culture, God is glorified and the nations of the earth are forever transformed.

Christians from ten countries met in London in 1846 for the purpose of launching, in their own words, "a new thing in church history, a definite organization for the expression of unity amongst Christian individuals belonging to different churches." This was the beginning of a vision that was fulfilled in 1951 when believers from 21 countries officially formed the World Evangelical Fellowship. Today, 150 years after the London gathering, WEA is a dynamic global structure for unity and action that embraces 600 million evangelicals in 129 countries. It is a unity based on the historic Christian faith expressed in the evangelical tradition. And it looks to the future with vision to accomplish God's purposes in discipling the nations for Jesus Christ.

Commissions:

- Theology
- Missions
- Religious Liberty
- Women's Concerns
- Youth
- Information Technology

Initiatives and Activities

- Ambassador for Human Rights
- Ambassador for Refugees
- Creation Care Task Force
- Global Generosity Network
- International Institute for Religious Freedom
- International Institute for Islamic Studies
- Leadership Institute
- Micah Challenge
- Global Human Trafficking Task Force
- Peace and Reconciliation Initiative
- UN-Team

Church Street Station
P.O. Box 3402
New York, NY 10008-3402
Phone +[1] 212 233 3046
Fax +[1] 646-957-9218
www.worldea.org

Giving Hands

GIVING HANDS GERMANY (GH) was established in 1995 and is officially recognized as a nonprofit foreign aid organization. It is an international operating charity that – up to now – has been supporting projects in about 40 countries on four continents. In particular we care for orphans and street children. Our major focus is on Africa and Central America. GIVING HANDS always mainly provides assistance for self-help and furthers human rights thinking.

The charity itself is not bound to any church, but on the spot we are cooperating with churches of all denominations. Naturally we also cooperate with other charities as well as governmental organizations to provide assistance as effective as possible under the given circumstances.

The work of GIVING HANDS GERMANY is controlled by a supervisory board. Members of this board are Manfred Feldmann, Colonel V. Doner and Kathleen McCall. Dr. Christine Schirrmacher is registered as legal manager of GIVING HANDS at the local district court. The local office and work of the charity are coordinated by Rev. Horst J. Kreie as executive manager. Dr. theol. Thomas Schirrmacher serves as a special consultant for all projects.

Thanks to our international contacts companies and organizations from many countries time and again provide containers with gifts in kind which we send to the different destinations where these goods help to satisfy elementary needs. This statutory purpose is put into practice by granting nutrition, clothing, education, construction and maintenance of training centers at home and abroad, construction of wells and operation of water treatment systems, guidance for self-help and transportation of goods and gifts to areas and countries where needy people live.

GIVING HANDS has a publishing arm under the leadership of Titus Vogt, that publishes human rights and other books in English, Spanish, Swahili and other languages.

These aims are aspired to the glory of the Lord according to the basic Christian principles put down in the Holy Bible.

Baumschulallee 3a • D-53115 Bonn • Germany
Phone: +49 / 228 / 695531 • Fax +49 / 228 / 695532
www.gebende-haende.de • info@gebende-haende.de

 # Martin Bucer Seminary

Faithful to biblical truth
Cooperating with the Evangelical Alliance
Reformed

Solid training for the Kingdom of God
- Alternative theological education
- Study while serving a church or working another job
- Enables students to remain in their own churches
- Encourages independent thinking
- Learning from the growth of the universal church.

Academic
- For the Bachelor's degree: 180 Bologna-Credits
- For the Master's degree: 120 additional Credits
- Both old and new teaching methods: All day seminars, independent study, term papers, etc.

Our Orientation:
- Complete trust in the reliability of the Bible
- Building on reformation theology
- Based on the confession of the German Evangelical Alliance
- Open for innovations in the Kingdom of God

Our Emphasis:
- The Bible
- Ethics and Basic Theology
- Missions
- The Church

Our Style:
- Innovative
- Relevant to society
- International
- Research oriented
- Interdisciplinary

Structure
- 15 study centers in 7 countries with local partners
- 5 research institutes
- President: Prof. Dr. Thomas Schirrmacher
  Vice President: Prof. Dr. Thomas K. Johnson
- Deans: Thomas Kinker, Th.D.;
  Titus Vogt, lic. theol., Carsten Friedrich, M.Th.

Missions through research
- Institute for Religious Freedom
- Institute for Islamic Studies
- Institute for Life and Family Studies
- Institute for Crisis, Dying, and Grief Counseling
- Institute for Pastoral Care

www.bucer.eu • info@bucer.eu

Berlin | Bielefeld | Bonn | Chemnitz | Hamburg | Munich | Pforzheim
Innsbruck | Istanbul | Izmir | Linz | Prague | São Paulo | Tirana | Zurich

www.ingramcontent.com/pod-product-compliance
Lightning Source LLC
Chambersburg PA
CBHW051659090426
42736CB00013B/2447